2021

ausgerechnet

Training Quali

Original-Prüfungsaufgaben

Bayern

Englisch

LÖSUNGEN

STARK

© 2020 Stark Verlag GmbH
15. ergänzte Auflage
www.stark-verlag.de

Das Werk und alle seine Bestandteile sind urheberrechtlich geschützt. Jede vollständige oder teilweise Vervielfältigung, Verbreitung und Veröffentlichung bedarf der ausdrücklichen Genehmigung des Verlages. Dies gilt insbesondere für Vervielfältigungen, Mikroverfilmungen sowie die Speicherung und Verarbeitung in elektronischen Systemen.

Inhalt

Vorwort

Übungsaufgaben – Lösungen zum Kompetenzbereich „Listening" 1
Test 1: In the supermarket 1
Test 2: At the airport 2
Test 3: Mrs Brown at the shoe store 5
Test 4: Visit to Stirling Castle 7

Übungsaufgaben – Lösungen zum Kompetenzbereich „Use of English" 12

Übungsaufgaben – Lösungen zum Kompetenzbereich „Reading" 24
Test 1: Treasure hunting at the Florida Keys 24
Test 2: Camels in Australia 26
Test 3: Is autonomous driving becoming a reality? 27
Test 4: Kelechi Iheanacho 29

Übungsaufgaben – Lösungen zum Kompetenzbereich „Text Production" 31

Übungsaufgaben – Lösungen zum Kompetenzbereich „Speaking" 43

Lösungen Original-Prüfungsaufgaben
Quali 2012 .... E 2012-1
Quali 2013 .... E 2013-1
Quali 2014 .... E 2014-1
Quali 2015 .... E 2015-1
Quali 2016 .... E 2016-1
Quali 2017 .... E 2017-1
Quali 2018 .... E 2018-1
Quali 2019 .... E 2019-1

Quali 2020 .... www.stark-verlag.de/mystark

Das Corona-Virus hat im vergangenen Schuljahr auch die Prüfungsabläufe durcheinandergebracht und manches verzögert. Daher sind die Lösungen zur **Prüfung 2020** in diesem Jahr nicht in diesem Buch abgedruckt, sondern erscheinen in digitaler Form. Sobald die Original-Prüfungsaufgaben 2020 zur Veröffentlichung freigegeben sind, kannst du das **PDF** auf der Plattform **MyStark** herunterladen.

Autorin: Birgit Mohr

Vorwort

Liebe Schülerin, lieber Schüler,

dieses Buch enthält die Lösungen zu dem Band **Training Quali Englisch Bayern** (Bestellnummer 93555/93555ML).
Die Lösungen bzw. Lösungsvorschläge in diesem Buch ermöglichen es dir, deine Leistung einzuschätzen. Durch die **Hinweise** zu einzelnen Aufgaben lernst du, was bei einer bestimmten Aufgabenstellung von dir erwartet wird.

Viel Erfolg im Quali wünscht dir

Birgit Mohr

Übungsaufgaben
Lösungen zum Kompetenzbereich „Listening"

✏ **Allgemeiner Hinweis:** *Zum Lösen aller folgenden Aufgaben zum Kapitel „Listening" musst du dir den Text jeweils genau anhören. Wenn du ihn nach dem ersten Hören noch nicht verstanden hast, kannst du ihn dir natürlich auch öfter anhören. Lies dir den Hörverstehenstext nur durch, wenn du mit den Lösungen ganz unsicher bist und gar nicht weiterkommst.*

Listening Comprehension Test 1: In the supermarket

1   Dear customers, welcome to Richie's Supermarket, where you can always get a bargain!
    This week we are celebrating health week at Richie's Supermarket, and we take special care to offer you the best products for the health of your whole family at
5   the best prices you can find!
    In our fruit and vegetable department, you can pick your choice of the best apples, pears or tomatoes for just 59 pence per kilo! Yes, that's one kilo of apples, pears or tomatoes for just 59 pence! By the way, the 5 kilogram bag of potatoes now costs only 1 pound 79.
10 Or, if you are looking for some relaxing moments, why don't you visit our cosmetics department, where you will find a wide selection of natural bath products for just 99 pence each. Imagine, you can take a refreshing, relaxing bath, with the fragrance of your choice, for just 99 pence! What's more, all sun lotions are now reduced by 25 %.
15 Dear customers, at Richie's Supermarket we care for your health. Take your time to find out about our offers, and enjoy your health week with us!

Aufgabe 1

a) Richie's
   ✏ Hinweis: Z. 1
b) health week
   ✏ Hinweis: Z. 3

Aufgabe 2

a) 59 pence
   ✏ Hinweis: Z. 6 f.

b) 1 pound 79 pence
   🖉 Hinweis: Z. 8 f.
c) 99 pence
   🖉 Hinweis: Z. 11 f.
d) 25 %
   🖉 Hinweis: Z. 13 f.

Aufgabe 3

a) *wrong:* protests, *correct:* products
b) *wrong:* friend, *correct:* fruit
c) *wrong:* normal, *correct:* natural
d) *wrong:* money, *correct:* time

Listening Comprehension Test 2: At the airport

Part 1: At the check-in

Mr Miller: Good afternoon, my wife and I have tickets to Munich. I hope we are not too late for the flight.
Woman at service desk: Please give me your tickets and your passports.
Mr Miller: Here they are.
Woman at service desk: Thank you. OK, let me check ...
Woman at service desk: Mr and Mrs Miller – you are going to Munich via Frankfurt?
Mr Miller: Yes, we have to change planes in Frankfurt.
Woman at service desk: OK, you are still on time for the flight to Frankfurt. But you have to hurry – the plane is going to take off in 20 minutes! Where would you like to sit in the plane, by the window or on the aisle?
Mr Miller: On the aisle, please.
Woman at service desk: No problem. I am giving you two seats in the centre row – one of them is next to the aisle. Would you like to check in any luggage?
Mr Miller: No, thanks, we have only hand luggage.
Woman at service desk: OK.
Woman at service desk: Here are your boarding cards to Frankfurt, and from Frankfurt to Munich. Please proceed to Gate 17 immediately.
Mr Miller: Thank you.
Woman at service desk: Enjoy your flight!

Aufgabe 1

a) true
   Hinweis: Z. 2
b) false
   Hinweis: Z. 4 f.
c) false
   Hinweis: Z. 13
d) false
   Hinweis: Z. 16

Aufgabe 2

a) their tickets and passports
   Hinweis: Z. 4
b) in Frankfurt
   Hinweis: Z. 9
c) in 20 minutes
   Hinweis: Z. 11
d) 17
   Hinweis: Z. 19

Part 2: Boarding the plane
(Busy sounds of passengers boarding the plane)
Woman: Excuse me, sir?
Mr Miller: Who? Me?
Woman: Yes, sir. Excuse me, I'm sorry to bother you but it looks like you are sitting in my seat.
Mr Miller: Oh, really? Let me check our boarding cards …
(Rustling in his travel bag.)
Mr Miller: Hmm, where are they … just a moment.
Woman: Sure, no hurry.
Mr Miller: Ah, here they are. Let me just check … Here, please take a look, my wife and I have seats 21D and 21E. Which seat do you have?
Woman: Oops, that's strange. My seat number is 21E, too!
Mr Miller: This is very strange. It must be the airline's mistake!
Woman *(sighing)*: It must be! Wait a moment, I'm just going to ask the flight attendant.
(Some time passes.)

Flight attendant: Hello, sir! This lady tells me that you have the same seat as she does. Could you please show me your boarding cards?
Mr Miller: Yes, of course. Here, these are the boarding cards for my wife and myself.
Flight attendant: 21D and 21E ... Mr and Mrs Miller ... The flight number and date are correct. You really are sitting in the right seat. Could you show me your boarding card again, please?
Woman: OK, here it is.
Flight attendant: Ah, that's it! This boarding card is for another flight. Look, it has the same flight number, but the date was two weeks ago! Did you travel to Frankfurt two weeks ago, too?
Woman: Oh, yes, you're right, excuse me. This is my fault, it's the wrong boarding card. I travel to Frankfurt every two weeks and that's an old one. Let me just check in my bag ...
Flight attendant: No problem for you, Mr and Mrs Miller, you have the right seats.
Mr Miller: OK, thank you.
Woman: I'm afraid I can't find my boarding card, I don't know where I put it.
Flight attendant: That's no problem. Please come with me and I will look up your seat on the computer. *(Voice fading)* It's not the first time that somebody lost their boarding card on the way from the gate to the plane ...

Aufgabe 3

a) B
   ◢ Hinweis: *Z. 5 f.*
b) A
   ◢ Hinweis: *Z. 14*
c) C
   ◢ Hinweis: *Z. 22 f.*
d) C
   ◢ Hinweis: *Z. 26*
e) B
   ◢ Hinweis: *Z. 34*

Aufgabe 4

a) 21E
b) (the) boarding card(s)
c) 2/two weeks before/ago

d) (on the) computer

Listening Comprehension Test 3: Mrs Brown at the shoe store

Part 1
Shop assistant: Hello, how can I help you?
Mrs Brown: Hello, I'm looking for a pair of shoes for the summer.
Shop assistant: Do you have something specific in mind?
Mrs Brown *(hesitantly)*: Mm, yes. I'd like a pair of comfortable leather shoes.
Shop assistant: What colour are you looking for?
Mrs Brown: A light colour please, maybe white or beige.
Shop assistant: OK, please come over to our summer section.

Aufgabe 1
a) summer
   ✏ Hinweis: Z. 3
b) comfortable
   ✏ Hinweis: Z. 5
c) beige
   ✏ Hinweis: Z. 7

Part 2
Shop assistant: Here, take a look at this pair. They are a new design from Italy and are very comfortable. Are these the type of shoes you like to wear?
Mrs Brown: Not exactly. These shoes are too high – I don't think I could wear them for more than an hour. I also don't like it that my toes show. I'd like a closed pair of shoes that I can wear with socks.
Shop assistant: Of course. Please come over to this aisle, where we have the more casual shoes.
Shop assistant *(after a moment)*: Here, please have a look. What do you think of these loafers, which are a nice beige? These are from another collection from Italy.
Mrs Brown: Oh, yes, they do look nice! I think I'd like to try them.
Shop assistant: What size can I get for you?
Mrs Brown: That would be a 5, thank you.

Aufgabe 2

a) toes
   Hinweis: Z. 5
b) socks
   Hinweis: Z. 6
c) Italy
   Hinweis: Z. 10 ff.

Part 3

Shop assistant: How do the shoes fit? Do they feel comfortable?
Mrs Brown: Phew, I'm afraid they don't fit. Have you got them half a size larger?
Shop assistant: One moment, I'll go to the back again to look. I'm not sure that we still have this style in 5 ½, I think we've already sold all of them. *(pause while he goes to look)*
Mrs Brown: And, have you got them in 5 ½?
Shop assistant: Sorry, I'm afraid not. Size 5 ½ is completely sold out. But I did bring you a size 6. Would you like to have a try?
Mrs Brown: Oh, that's a pity ... but OK, I'll try them.
Mrs Brown *(after a moment)*: Let's see ...
Shop assistant: What do you think, do they fit nicely?
Mrs Brown: Yes, I think they do fit! But I'm a bit surprised that I'm a size 6 now!
Shop assistant: Don't worry, this make is sometimes a bit tighter than others.
Mrs Brown: OK ... Well, I've made up my mind – I would like to buy these shoes.
Shop assistant: Perfect!

Aufgabe 3

a) fit
   Hinweis: Z. 3
b) 5.5/5 ½
   Hinweis: Z. 3 ff.
c) 6
   Hinweis: Z. 13 ff.

Part 4

1 **Girl at cash register:** Hello, how are you today? What would you like to pay for?
Mrs Brown: That pair of beige loafers, please.
Girl at cash register: OK.
5 **Girl at cash register:** That'll be forty-nine ninety-five. Would you like to pay by cash or credit card?
Mrs Brown: I'd like to pay by credit card, please. Here you are.
Girl at cash register: Thanks!
Girl at cash register: So, here are your shoes. Thanks very much. Goodbye now.
10 **Mrs Brown:** Thanks. Goodbye!

Aufgabe 4

a) true
   ✎ Hinweis: Z. 3
b) false
   ✎ Hinweis: Z. 5
c) true
   ✎ Hinweis: Z. 7

Listening Comprehension Test 4: Visit to Stirling Castle

1 **Part 1**
(Conversation starts between two teenagers on back seat of a car)
Tabby: Nick, you've been playing that game for hours now, could you please turn it off?
5 **Nick** *(sounding absent)*: No.
Tabby: Nick, please! I don't want to hear that sound anymore. Could you turn it off, now!?
Nick *(concentrating on his game)*: Sorry, Tabby, I can't turn it off, now ... I have to finish this level first.
10 **Tabby:** Please!
Nick *(after a moment)*: There you go, I finally made it to level fourteen! Wow! *(pause)*
Nick: What a bummer, it looks like the rain out there is never going to end. Anyway, do you know where Mum and Dad are driving us to?
15 **Tabby:** Sure, I've been reading all about it in this travel guide, while you were playing that stupid game. We're driving to Stirling Castle – ever heard of it?

Nick: Yes, I think we learned about Stirling Castle in history class. Isn't it the most important castle in Scotland?
Tabby: Yes, it is. It's one of the largest and most important castles of the country. Several Scottish kings and queens were crowned at Stirling Castle, for example Mary, Queen of Scots, in 1543. She also lived there with her family.
Nick: Was that the same queen as Mary Stuart?
Tabby: Yes, Mary, Queen of Scots, and Mary Stuart were the same person. Didn't you know that? Anyway, did you know that when Mary, Queen of Scots, was crowned she was still a baby?
Nick: No, really?
Tabby: Yes. That was because her father, King James V, died shortly after she was born.
Nick: Hmmm ... interesting. What else does your travel guide tell us about Stirling Castle?
Tabby: Here ... Did you know that many people claim to have seen ghosts at Stirling Castle?
Nick: Really? That sounds cool.
Tabby: Yes. Listen to this: Several ghosts have reportedly been seen at Stirling Castle. The one seen most often is the so-called Highland Ghost. He was seen by both staff and visitors, and he was wearing a traditional Scottish costume. Some tourists first thought he was a tour guide, but then they saw him turn around, walk away and vanish in front of their eyes!
Nick: Wow!
Tabby: And listen to this *(reading excitedly)*: The Green Lady is another famous ghost in Stirling Castle. The legend is that she was a servant girl to Mary, Queen of Scots. One night while the queen was sleeping, and the servant girl was with her, the curtains of the queen's bed caught fire from a candle. Although she was able to save the queen's life, the servant girl was badly injured and died. Ever since, from time to time, a ghost has been seen in the castle, wearing green clothes – the same colour as the servant girl's clothes. This is why the ghost is called the Green Lady. And there are still some more ghosts ...
Nick: Aha. Well, Tabby, let's see if we can find some of them at the castle ...
Tabby *(giving Nick a punch)*: Stop it, Nick, you're so dumb. I'm frightened by all of these stories already!

Aufgabe 1

a) Scotland
   Hinweis: Z. 17 f.

b) the same person.
   ✏ Hinweis: Z. 23
c) was still a baby.
   ✏ Hinweis: Z. 24 f.
d) "Highland Ghost".
   ✏ Hinweis: Z. 35 f.
e) was badly injured when saving the queen's life.
   ✏ Hinweis: Z. 42 ff.
f) clothes.
   ✏ Hinweis: Z. 45 f.

1 **Part 2**
   Tour guide: And now I would like to welcome you to the palace of Stirling Castle. It is one of the most remarkable Renaissance buildings in Britain. The palace was built in 1540 for King James V. The Scottish kings and queens used this
5 palace as a royal residence until 1603. In 1603, King James VI also became King of England, and the royal court moved to London.
   A few years ago, the palace of Stirling Castle was completely renovated for 12 million pounds. Artists from many countries made the interior look like it could have been in the 16th century, when Mary, Queen of Scots, was running
10 around in the palace as a young girl. So the paintings and pieces of furniture you see in this hall are not the originals from the 16th century. This is why they have such a beautiful, fresh colour. *(fading)*
   Nick *(whispers)*: Wow, Tabby, this is the greatest castle I've ever seen!
   Tabby *(whispers back)*: Haven't I told you?
15 **Nick:** Yeah …
   Tour guide *(fading in)*: In the castle you can also meet costumed characters, who demonstrate to the visitors what life in the palace and at the royal court was like in the 16th century. As you walk through the rooms, you will see servants, musicians, ambassadors and all sorts of characters.
20 **Nick** *(whispers)*: Cool, let's have a look and find some of these costumed characters.
   Tabby *(whispers back)*: Yes, let's try!

Aufgabe 2
a) in 1540
   ✏ Hinweis: Z. 3 f.

b) in 1603
    Hinweis: Z. 4 ff.
c) to London
    Hinweis: Z. 5 f.
d) 12 million pounds
    Hinweis: Z. 7 f.
e) artists (from many countries)
    Hinweis: Z. 8 f.
f) (the) 16th century
    Hinweis: Z. 16 ff.

Part 3

Nick: Here, Tabby, let's stand under this archway. It's really too bad we left the umbrella inside the car!

Tabby: I wonder where Mum and Dad are now. I hope they aren't looking for us ... Gosh, I'm all wet and cold!

Nick: I think they're still inside the palace, or in the souvenir shop. It's a pretty long tour, don't you think?

Tabby: Good for them, so they're at least inside! I told you we shouldn't have left the tour.

Nick: Let's go inside here for a moment. It's drier in there.

Tabby: Yes, it is.

Nick: Tabby, look!

Tabby: What?

Nick: There is another one of those costumed characters from the palace, over there in the shadow ... She looks like a servant.

Tabby: What? Where? I can't see anyone.

Nick: Right there! Don't you see her? She's carrying something ...

Tabby: *Where?* I don't see her!

Nick *(screams)*: Ahh!

Tabby: Nick, what happened? Did you step on something?

Nick: T ... T ... Tabby, you won't believe what I just saw!

Tabby *(frightened)*: What? What did you see?

Nick: T ... T ... The servant girl! Sh ... Sh ... She was standing there just a moment ago. She was carrying a basket or something. But then she just turned around and walked right into that wall.

Tabby *(screams)*: Ahh! What? Are you serious?

Nick: Yes! I ... I ... saw her ... She was wearing a green dress and a white apron ...

Tabby: Oh my God! Let's get out of here!
Nick: Right, let's leave this place!
30 **Tabby:** Oh my God! This is scary!!!

Aufgabe 3

0	1	2	3	4
A	C	D	G	I

1 **Part 4**
(In the car)
Tabby: You are such an idiot! I'll never tell you anything about any place we visit, ever again.
5 **Nick:** *(laughing)*
Tabby: You idiot!
Nick *(laughing)*: Sorry, it was just so funny … you should have seen your face. The moment I told you the costumed servant disappeared into the wall …
Tabby: Stop it! I hate you!
10 **Nick:** *(laughing)*
Tabby: For a moment I really believed you and thought there was a ghost!
Nick: *(laughing)* That was funny, wasn't it?
Tabby: Don't ever, ever do that again!
Nick: OK, I won't.
15 **Tabby:** Promise?
Nick: Sure, I promise. *(cracks up again and continues to laugh)*
Tabby: Ahh! I don't believe you! I swear I will NEVER go into ANY castle with you again!

Aufgabe 4

a) *wrong:* idiom, *correct:* idiot
b) *wrong:* teach, *correct:* tell
c) *wrong:* not, *correct:* just
d) *wrong:* trusted, *correct:* believed
e) *wrong:* palace, *correct:* castle

Übungsaufgaben
Lösungen zum Kompetenzbereich „Use of English"

Aufgabe 1

Beispiellösungen:
a) At school you find chalk, <u>a blackboard</u> and <u>pupils</u>, for example.
b) When it is cold in winter there is <u>snow</u> and <u>ice</u>.
c) In the zoo there are a lot of animals, for example <u>monkeys</u>, <u>tigers</u> and <u>bears</u>.

Aufgabe 2

Beispiellösungen:

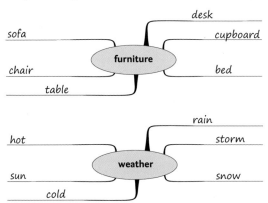

Aufgabe 3

✏ **Hinweis:** *In dieser Aufgabe ist der Oberbegriff nicht vorgegeben. Du musst überlegen, was die aufgelisteten Wörter bzw. die Bilder gemeinsam haben.*
a) colours/colors
b) vehicles
c) languages

Aufgabe 4

✏ Hinweis: *Zu Beginn jeder Zeile ist der Oberbegriff vorgegeben. Du musst also nur noch überlegen, welches Wort nicht dazu passt.*

a) pineapple
   ✏ Hinweis: *kein Gemüse*
b) horse
   ✏ Hinweis: *kein Fahrzeug*
c) vinegar
   ✏ Hinweis: *kein Getränk*
d) fork
   ✏ Hinweis: *keine Mahlzeit*
e) soft
   ✏ Hinweis: *keine Geschmacksrichtung*

Aufgabe 5

✏ Hinweis: *Hier musst du überlegen, welches Wort nicht in die Reihe passt, und was die verbliebenen Wörter gemeinsam haben.*

a) ~~bag~~ → clothes
   ✏ Hinweis: *„bag" ist kein Kleidungsstück*
b) ~~pen~~ → car/bus/van/vehicles
   ✏ Hinweis: *„pen" ist kein Teil eines Fahrzeugs*
c) ~~food~~ → parts of the body
   ✏ Hinweis: *„food" ist kein Körperteil*
d) ~~knife~~ → vegetables
   ✏ Hinweis: *„knife" ist kein Gemüse*
e) ~~meat~~ → desserts
   ✏ Hinweis: *„meat" ist kein Nachtisch*

Aufgabe 6

a) restaurant
b) theatre
c) hospital
d) church
e) park

Aufgabe 7

board	–	bored
whole	–	hole
no	–	know
break	–	brake
hour	–	our
piece	–	peace
see	–	sea

Aufgabe 8

a) It was dark at • <u>in</u> • over the morning when I went to school.

b) The plane was left • <u>late</u> • soon this morning.

c) I often drive • <u>go</u> • miss by train.

d) What • Which • <u>Where</u> can I buy a watch, please?

Aufgabe 9

Aufgabe 10

⚠ **Hinweis:** *Im Englischen haben nur wenige Nomen eine eigene „weibliche" Form. Oft wird das Nomen (z. B. „teacher" = „Lehrer"/„Lehrerin") durch ein Pronomen (z. B. „he"/„his" oder „she"/„her") oder eine Ergänzung (z. B. „Mrs/Ms", „Mr") näher bestimmt, sodass klar ist, ob es sich um eine weibliche oder männliche Person handelt.*

a) policewoman
b) princess
c) actress
d) waitress

Aufgabe 11

a) knives
b) mice
c) men
d) women
e) children
f) fish
g) leaves
h) teeth

Aufgabe 12

a) railway station
b) travel agency
c) suitcase
d) passport

Aufgabe 13

a) a radio
b) a pen
c) a mobile phone
d) a key

Aufgabe 14

a) Big Ben is a tourist a<u>ttraction</u> in London.

b) The "Anne Frank House" is in Amsterdam. That is in the Netherlands. The people there are called the **D**<u>utch</u>.

c) The Leaning Tower of Pisa is in Italy. The people there **s**p<u>eak</u> Italian.

d) The Eiffel Tower is in Paris. Paris is the **c**ap<u>ital</u> of France.

e) The Puerta del Sol is in Madrid, in Spain. People from Spain are called **S**p<u>anish</u>.

Aufgabe 15

🖊 **Hinweis:** *Die Antworten geben dir Aufschluss darüber, welches Fragewort du verwenden musst.*

a) <u>Where</u> is the cafeteria?

b) <u>How much</u> is a sandwich?

c) <u>Who</u> is that girl over there?

d) <u>Why</u> is she looking so sad?

e) <u>When</u> did she move?

Aufgabe 16

🖊 **Hinweis:** *Zur Kontrolle, ob du die Lücken korrekt ausgefüllt hast, lies dir am Ende den gesamten Text noch einmal durch. Wenn du merkst, dass manche Sätze keinen Sinn ergeben, musst du dir andere Lösungsmöglichkeiten überlegen.*

a) **Clara:** Hi Eric, how <u>are</u> you?

b) **Eric:** <u>Fine</u>, thanks. How are you?

c) **Clara:** I'm fine, too. But I <u>miss</u> you all.

d) **Eric:** We miss you, too. <u>When</u> are you coming home?

e) **Clara:** <u>On</u> Friday.

f) **Eric:** We're looking forward <u>to</u> seeing you.

Aufgabe 17

🖊 **Hinweis:** *Hier musst du nicht auf die Verwendung der richtigen Zeit achten, da alle Verben in der Grundform (Infinitiv) eingesetzt werden.*

"I'm going to <u>wear</u> my suit and I <u>think</u> I will be very nervous. I <u>hope</u> I won't <u>forget</u> my lines. Even my grandparents <u>want</u> to come and <u>see</u> me acting. I hope everyone will <u>enjoy</u> the evening."

Aufgabe 18

Sara: "Lisa and I are going <u>to</u> Paris on 12th May."
Pierre: "When <u>will</u> you arrive in Paris?"
Sara: "At 2.35 pm."
Pierre: "<u>What</u> is the name of the hotel you're staying at?"
Sara: "<u>It's</u> Hôtel de Paris."
Pierre: "Do you have any <u>plans</u> for your stay?"
Sara: "I want to do some <u>shopping</u>/<u>sightseeing</u> and visit the Eiffel Tower and the Champs-Elysées."
Pierre: "I would like <u>to show you</u> the nightlife in Paris. I'm looking <u>forward</u> to seeing you next <u>week</u>."

Aufgabe 19

Hinweis: Für die Verwendung der Präpositionen gibt es keine festen Regeln. Am besten lernst du die jeweiligen Präpositionen immer zusammen mit den entsprechenden Verben. In der Grammatik findest du auf Seite 81 ff. eine Übersicht über häufige Präpositionen im Englischen.

a) The teacher is sitting <u>at</u> the table.
b) Jessica has never been <u>to</u> Australia.
c) What do you think <u>of</u> my new dress?
d) The new boy in our class is <u>from</u> Singapore.
e) I am waiting <u>for</u> you at the bus stop.

Aufgabe 20

Hinweis: Das Present progressive findest du auf Seite 87 in der Grammatik.

a) What are you <u>doing</u> in this picture?
b) I <u>am carrying</u> a large watermelon I bought at the market.
c) The dress I <u>am wearing</u> in this picture is new.
d) The sun <u>is shining</u> in every picture.
e) Here we <u>are going</u> down to the beach.

Aufgabe 21

✏ **Hinweis:** *Die Regeln zur Verwendung des Going-to-future kannst du in der Grammatik auf Seite 90 nachlesen.*

a) I <u>am going to meet</u> Jane on Saturday for breakfast.
b) On Monday I <u>am going to see</u> the doctor.
c) I <u>am going to go</u> camping with some of my friends.

Aufgabe 22

✏ **Hinweis:** *Das Simple past findest du auf Seite 88 der Grammatik.*

On Saturday morning Kelly and Sara <u>met</u> in town to do some shopping. They <u>were</u> invited to a birthday party in the evening and <u>wanted</u> to buy a present. At first they <u>couldn't</u> really decide what to buy, but then they <u>saw</u> a cool smartphone case and <u>were</u> sure that that would be the right present for Tim. Now they <u>could</u> take a look around for some trendy clothes for the party. Kelly <u>bought</u> a T-shirt, but Sara <u>didn't</u> find anything. Afterwards they <u>went</u> home to get changed for the party.

Aufgabe 23

✏ **Hinweis:** *Hier musst du entscheiden, welche Zeitform korrekt ist. Signalwörter, z.B. „yesterday", „now" „last week", helfen dir dabei, die richtige Zeit anzuwenden. Du kannst dazu noch einmal alle Regeln in der Grammatik ab Seite 86 nachlesen.*

a) I <u>felt</u> very sick yesterday, so I went to bed early and now <u>I'm feeling</u>/<u>I feel</u> much better.
b) In 1982, my brother <u>was</u> born.
c) I <u>am going to move</u>/I <u>am moving</u> to Australia in October. I can't stand the English weather any longer.
d) My aunt <u>gave</u> me this book for my birthday last week.

Aufgabe 24

a) <u>Do you have</u> tickets for the Rihanna concert?
b) No, I'm sorry. We <u>sold</u> the last one yesterday.
c) What a pity! But what about the open air festival which <u>takes place</u> in August?
d) Yes, we <u>still have</u> tickets for the festival.

Aufgabe 25

1	2	3	4
C	A	D	B

Aufgabe 26

🖋 **Hinweis:** *Adverbien beschreiben u. a., auf welche Art und Weise etwas geschieht.*

a) gladly
b) easily
c) well
d) closely

Aufgabe 27

🖋 **Hinweis:** *Die Signalwörter für die Verwendung des Simple present findest du auf Seite 87 in der Grammatik. Beachte bei der Bildung des Simple present den Merksatz: „He, she, it – ‚s' muss mit!"*

a) Mum <u>always</u> **wakes** me up in the morning.
b) Sally <u>often</u> **goes** hiking at the weekends.
c) <u>Every year</u>, Mr Jones **spends** his holidays in Ireland.
d) <u>On Mondays</u>, Jane **is** <u>always</u> late for school. The rest of the week she <u>usually</u> **arrives** on time.
e) Lisa <u>never</u> **does** her <u>homework</u> properly.

Aufgabe 28

🖋 **Hinweis:** *Die Regeln zur Steigerung von Adjektiven findest du auf Seite 84 f. der Grammatik.*

a) Jessica is <u>taller</u> than Jenny.
b) Jim is <u>the tallest</u> boy in our class.
c) Sara has <u>the longest/(long)</u> hair.
d) Michelle's hair is <u>darker</u> than Tina's.
e) Toby is <u>better</u> at playing football than Mark.
f) But Lisa is the <u>best</u> player!

Aufgabe 29

▸ **Hinweis:** *Entscheide auch hier, ob du die 1. oder die 2. Steigerungsform einsetzen musst. Hinzu kommt auch der Vergleich mit „as ... as".*

Danny:
The weather in France was much <u>worse</u> than last year. It was raining almost all the time. Our flat, however, was <u>more comfortable</u> than last year. I also like the French food. It's much <u>better</u> than the food in England. In my opinion, France is the <u>most beautiful</u> country in Europe.

Luisa:
I went to Spain with a youth group. The weather in San Sebastian was almost as <u>bad as</u> in France, but it was <u>more exciting</u> to spend the holidays there than with my parents in Scotland. In my opinion, Spanish food is the <u>best</u> in Europe. My holiday in Spain was great, and I met <u>more</u> people <u>than</u> in all my holidays before!

Aufgabe 30

▸ **Hinweis:** *Hier musst du die fehlenden Pronomen (Fürwörter) einsetzen. Die Regeln zur Verwendung von Pronomen findest du auf Seite 75 der Grammatik.*

Mrs Brown comes into the classroom, looks out of the window and asks her class in surprise, "Whose jacket is that lying outside?" John answers, "<u>It</u> is Lisa's." "Lisa, is that true? Is that y<u>ou</u>r jacket?" Mrs Brown asks. "Go and get <u>it</u>, please." Then Mrs Brown notices that Lisa is not in the classroom. "Where is <u>she</u> today?" "<u>I</u> think <u>she</u> is ill," says Maggie, who sounds as if she has been crying, "<u>She</u> didn't wait for <u>me</u> this morning like <u>she</u> usually does. <u>I</u> borrowed <u>her</u> jacket yesterday and <u>she</u> told me to look after <u>it</u>. But this morning, Jack and Tim took the jacket and threw <u>it</u> around. <u>I</u> couldn't catch <u>it</u>, and then <u>they</u> threw <u>it</u> out of the window." "Is that true, y<u>ou</u> two?" asks Mrs Brown, "Did y<u>ou</u> do that? Go and get the jacket immediately, give <u>it</u> back to Maggie and say sorry to <u>her</u>. <u>You</u> will stay behind after school and clean up the classroom." Jack is very angry and says, "<u>It</u> wasn't <u>me</u>!" <u>He</u> points at Tim: "<u>He</u> did it – <u>it</u> was all <u>his</u> fault!" Mrs Brown turns to the whole class and says, "All of y<u>ou</u> saw <u>them</u> take the jacket and throw <u>it</u> out of the window, and did any of y<u>ou</u> help Maggie? No, y<u>ou</u> didn't. <u>I</u> have decided that y<u>ou</u> will all stay behind after school and clean up the classroom. Maggie, y<u>ou</u> go to Lisa's house straight after school, return the jacket to <u>her</u> and explain what <u>we</u>/ <u>they</u> did at school today. And now, everyone, please show <u>me</u> y<u>ou</u>r homework!"

Aufgabe 31

✏ **Hinweis:** *Die Regeln zu den Relativsätzen und zur Verwendung der Relativpronomen kannst du in der Grammatik auf Seite 83 f. nachlesen.*

a) Doesn't the pullover <u>which</u> is lying on the floor belong to you?
b) The man <u>who</u> lives next door had an accident yesterday.
c) The book <u>which</u> you lent me last week was really exciting.
d) The woman <u>who</u> is sitting next to you is my mother.
e) The train <u>which</u> arrived late was very crowded.

Aufgabe 32

✏ **Hinweis:** *Die Regeln zu den if-clauses kannst du auf den Seiten 74 f. nachlesen.*

a) If I take the train, I <u>will be</u> late.
b) If you don't take an umbrella with you, you <u>will get</u> wet.
c) If I move to America, I <u>will improve</u> my English.
d) I <u>won't tell</u> you, even if you ask me a hundred times.

Aufgabe 33

a) I would like a loaf of bread, please.
b) Could you tell me the way to the next bus station?
c) I'd like to have the menu, please.
d) Do you have this pair of jeans one size bigger?

Aufgabe 34

✏ **Hinweis:** *Die Regeln zur Wortstellung kannst du auf Seite 86 in der Grammatik nachlesen.*

a) Paul is going to visit his aunt and uncle in California.
b) They invited him to spend the summer with them.
c) Zoe is jealous that her brother is going to make a trip.
d) Zoe's aunt promises that she can visit them soon, too.

Aufgabe 35

a) Where are you from?/Where do you live?
b) How old are you?
c) Why are you here?
d) Do you like it here?/Do you like this town?
e) Have you ever been here before?

Aufgabe 36

🖊 **Hinweis:** *Die Regeln zur Bildung der Verneinung findest du auf Seite 86 ff.*

a) The sun <u>isn't shining</u> outside.
b) Mr Weaver <u>didn't enjoy</u> the film he watched yesterday.
c) The Smiths <u>don't have</u>/<u>haven't got</u> a new car.
d) Sara <u>doesn't have</u>/<u>hasn't got</u> a dog.
e) The weather forecast says it <u>won't</u> rain tomorrow.
f) The Millers <u>aren't travelling</u> around Europe.

Aufgabe 37

🖊 **Hinweis:** *Lies zuerst den ganzen Text und versuche, den Inhalt trotz der Lücken zu erschließen. Konzentriere dich dann auf jeden einzelnen Satz. Dabei kann es hilfreich sein, die Sätze in deine Muttersprache zu übersetzen. Wenn dir das fehlende Wort eingefallen ist, überprüfe es noch einmal im Satzzusammenhang. So erkennst du, ob das Wort auch die richtige grammatikalische Form (z. B. Zeitform) hat.*

(1) ask questions = Fragen stellen; Signalwort „yesterday" → ask<u>ed</u> (Simple past)
(2) ask questions *about* = Fragen stellen <u>über</u>/<u>zu</u>
(3) subject = Unterrichtsfach
(4) there is = es gibt
(5) Relativpronomen „which/that" (welches, das) → bezieht sich auf das Football-Team; „who" kann sich nur auf Personen beziehen; oder: Konjunktion „*and*"
(6) how = wie
(7) be quite OK = ziemlich in Ordnung sein

Hi Brian,

Yesterday I met my tutor, Mr Castiello, (0) **at** school. He (1) **asked** me a lot of questions, for example (2) **about** my family or what it was like at my old school. He already knew that Maths is my favourite (3) **subject**, so I'm going to be in an honors class again. The good news: (4) **There** is a football team at the new school (5) **which/that/and** I can join right away. The next practice is already tomorrow afternoon. This is great! Let's see (6) **how** good this team is and what matches they have with other schools. Thinking about it, my new school could actually (7) **be** quite OK!

Take care,
Jason

Aufgabe 38

✏ **Hinweis:** *Lies erst den ganzen Text durch, um einen Eindruck zu gewinnen, wovon er handelt. Sollten dir hier schon Fehler auffallen, markiere sie. Gehe den Text dann Satz für Satz durch – die Fehler befinden sich übrigens immer in den Zeilen neben den Linien, auf die du das richtige Wort schreibst. Um das korrekte Wort zu finden, kann es hilfreich sein, die Sätze in deine Muttersprache zu übersetzen. Im Folgenden sind die richtigen Lösungen fett gedruckt.*

0. my = besitzanzeigendes Fürwort „mein"
1. in the middle *of* sth. = feststehender Ausdruck („mitten im Schuljahr")
2. Mrs Stephenson → *she*
3. 22 students = Mehrzahl → *are*
4. girls and boys = zählbare Namenwörter → *many*
5. Justin (= he) → live*s* (3. Person Singular: „he, she, it: -s muss mit")
6. will/are going to (Formen, die etwas Zukünftiges ausdrücken), can/could (modale Hilfsverben) → können hier mit „be" kombiniert werden

Dear diary,
Today was **0. my** (~~me~~) first day at the new school. It was OK. I was a bit nervous because I am joining a new class in the middle **1. of** (~~for~~) the year. All of the other students already know each other and I am the only new kid. But my new teacher, Mrs Stephenson, was really nice and **2. she** (~~he~~) introduced me to the whole class. There **3. are** (~~is~~) 22 students in the class, just about as **4. many** (~~much~~) girls as boys. I sit next to Justin, who also **5. lives** (~~live~~) in my neighborhood. Let's see, maybe we **6. will/are going to/can/could** (~~were~~) be friends.

Übungsaufgaben
Lösungen zum Kompetenzbereich „Reading"

🖉 **Allgemeiner Hinweis:** *In diesem Kapitel kannst du das Leseverstehen trainieren. Im Teil „Reading Comprehension" werden neben Fragen zum groben Verständnis auch Details abgefragt. Lies den Text deshalb besonders aufmerksam und nimm ihn immer wieder zur Hand, während du die zugehörigen Aufgaben bearbeitest. Verwende bei sprachlichen Unklarheiten auch das Wörterbuch.*

Reading Comprehension Test 1: Treasure hunting at the Florida Keys

Vokabelhinweise:
Z. 2 f.: *treasure hunter:* Schatzjäger
Z. 10: *dedication:* Hingabe
Z. 30: *goods:* hier: Frachtgut, Waren
Z. 37: *to remain:* bleiben
Z. 39: *to accompany:* begleiten
Z. 41 f.: *daughter-in-law:* Schwiegertochter
Z. 59: *cargo:* Fracht
Z. 63: *emerald:* Smaragd (ein Edelstein)
Z. 63: *artefacts:* Artefakte – hier: von Menschen hergestellte Gegenstände
Z. 83: *to be convinced:* überzeugt sein

Aufgabe 1

🖉 **Hinweis:** *Finde zu jedem Abschnitt die passende Überschrift. Eine Auswahl an Überschriften (A–G) ist vorgegeben. Wenn du die einzelnen Textabschnitte sorgfältig durchliest, wird es dir leichtfallen, die jeweils inhaltlich passende Überschrift zu finden.*

paragraph ❶ (lines 1–12)	C
paragraph ❷ (lines 13–27)	G
paragraph ❸ (lines 28–48)	E
paragraph ❹ (lines 49–68)	D
paragraph ❺ (lines 69–80)	A
paragraph ❻ (lines 81–90)	F

Aufgabe 2

	T	F	N
a) The *Atocha* was a Spanish ship.	✓		
b) Mel Fisher and his wife Dolores had a surf shop in California.		✓	
c) Mel and Dolores married in 1953.			✓

🖊 **Hinweis:** *Zwar haben Mel und Dolores im Jahr 1953 geheiratet, aber diese Information steht nicht im Text.*

	T	F	N
d) The *Atocha* was on her way to Havanna when she sank.		✓	
e) The treasure is worth about 40 million dollars.		✓	
f) You can also go on diving tours to the shipwreck site.	✓		

Aufgabe 3

🖊 **Hinweis:** *In der Aufgabe sind verschiedene Jahreszahlen angegeben. Finde im Text das Ereignis, das im jeweiligen Jahr stattfand.*

❶	❷	❸	❹	❺	❻	❼
H	B	F	D	G	C	E

Aufgabe 4

🖊 **Hinweis:** *Beantworte die Fragen anhand der Informationen aus dem Text. Es reicht, wenn du in Stichworten oder kurzen Sätzen antwortest.*

a) He had a "dive shop" and gave scuba diving trainings.
   🖊 **Hinweis:** *Z. 16 ff.*
b) 5/five
   🖊 **Hinweis:** *Z. 35 f.*
c) a (Spanish) ship/a sister ship of the *Atocha*
   🖊 **Hinweis:** *Z. 46 f.*
d) to make sure the treasures were collected properly/not damaged
   🖊 **Hinweis:** *Z. 65 ff.*
e) navigational instruments, military equipment, objects of native American origin, tools, ceramics, seeds, insects
   🖊 **Hinweis:** *Z. 75 ff.*

Reading Comprehension Test 2: Camels in Australia

Vokabelhinweise:
Z. 3: *annual: jährlich*
Z. 5: *scenery: Landschaft*
Z. 6: *cameleer: Kameltreiber/in*
Z. 8: *bet: Wette*
Z. 14: *to provide: (zur Verfügung) stellen*
Z. 48 f.: *Overland Telegraph Line: Telegrafenleitung, die durch ganz Australien gelegt wurde*
Z. 49 f.: *water supply infrastructure: Wasserversorgungsnetz*
Z. 58: *plant species: Pflanzenarten*
Z. 58 f.: *to pollute: verschmutzen*
Z. 72: *breeding: Zucht*

Aufgabe 1

a) Australia
   ✏ **Hinweis:** Z. 3
b) camel race.
   ✏ **Hinweis:** Z. 6 f.
c) made a bet with a friend.
   ✏ **Hinweis:** Z. 8 ff.
d) Australia.
   ✏ **Hinweis:** Z. 20 ff.
e) they can transport goods and are used to the heat.
   ✏ **Hinweis:** Z. 27 ff.
f) Australians spend a lot of money.
   ✏ **Hinweis:** Z. 61 ff.

Aufgabe 2

✏ **Hinweis:** *Im Lesetext fehlen verschiedene Sätze. Wähle für jede Lücke den passenden Satz aus und notiere den jeweiligen Buchstaben (A–G) in der Tabelle. Beachte, dass ein Satz in keine Lücke passt.*

❶	❷	❸	❹	❺	❻
E	D	A	G	C	F

Aufgabe 3

✏ **Hinweis:** Die Aufgabe enthält mehrere Aussagen, die alle sinngemäß im Lesetext zu finden sind. Suche nun die Stellen im Text, an denen diese Information vorkommen und gib die entsprechenden Zeilen an.

a) lines 10–12
b) lines 29/30
c) lines 32–34
d) lines 71/72

Aufgabe 4

✏ **Hinweis:** Hier reicht es, wenn du die Fragen mit kurzen Sätzen oder Stichworten beantwortest, die du dem Text entnehmen kannst.

a) up to 40 km
   ✏ *Hinweis: Z. 30 f.*
b) He was injured by his camel and died (because of the wounds).
   ✏ *Hinweis: Z. 39 ff.*
c) too many camels/eat 80 % of plant species/pollute water holes/damage water systems/they were set free
   ✏ *Hinweis: Z. 53 ff.*
d) export of live camels/export of camel meat/camel milk products
   ✏ *Hinweis: Z. 66 ff.*

Reading Comprehension Test 3: Is autonomous driving becoming a reality?

Vokabelhinweise:
Z. 3: *autonomous: eigenständig*
Z. 7: *driving license: Führerschein*
Z. 9: *to fail: versagen, ausfallen*
Z. 11 f.: *to be made responsible: verantwortlich gemacht werden*
Z. 15 f.: *intention: Absicht, Zweck*
Z. 17: *to increase: erhöhen*
Z. 19: *to request: hier: verlangen*
Z. 20: *measures: Maßnahmen*
Z. 29: *to improve: verbessern*
Z. 31: *to avoid: vermeiden*
Z. 40: *lane: Spur*
Z. 41: *blind spot: „toter Winkel"*

Z. 65: loss: Verlust
Z. 68: to blame sb: jmd. die Schuld geben
Z. 69: car manufacturer: Autohersteller
Z. 72: regulations: Vorschriften, Bestimmungen
Z. 81: to announce: ankündigen
Z. 89: to estimate: schätzen

Aufgabe 1

Hinweis: Ordne den Textabschnitten die richtige Überschrift zu. Beachte, dass drei Überschriften nicht passen und somit nicht zugeordnet werden können.

paragraph B	paragraph C	paragraph D	paragraph E	paragraph F
7	4	6	1	3

Aufgabe 2

Hinweis: Notiere die Aussagen, die mit den Informationen des Lesetextes übereinstimmen.

1. b
2. d
3. e
4. g
5. j

Aufgabe 3

Hinweis: Hier sind Aussagen aufgelistet, die inhaltlich alle im Text vorkommen, jedoch etwas anders formuliert sind als im Text selbst. Suche die entsprechenden Textstellen heraus und notiere, in welche(n) Zeile(n) diese stehen.

❶	❷	❸	❹	❺
line(s) 19–22	line(s) 38–40	line(s) 50–52	line(s) 63–65	line(s) 77–80

Aufgabe 4

✏ **Hinweis:** *Hier sind Wörter vorgegeben, die im Text vorkommen. Diese Wörter können unterschiedliche Bedeutungen haben. Lies auf S. 31 jedes Wort im Satzzusammenhang und finde heraus, welche deutsche Entsprechung jeweils Sinn ergibt.*

b) Fall   c) wichtigste/wesentliche   d) warnen   e) Führung

Reading Comprehension Test 4: Kelechi Iheanacho

Vokabelhinweise:

Z. 14: *to contribute:* beitragen
Z. 21 f.: *U-21 development squad:* hier: Mannschaft für unter 21-Jährige, die weiter aufgebaut werden sollen
Z. 46 f.: *Confederation of African Football:* Afrikanischer Fußballbund
Z. 50 f.: *to suggest:* hier: nahelegen, andeuten
Z. 52: *to aspire:* anstreben
Z. 55: *devotion:* Hingabe
Z. 55: *obstacle:* Hindernis
Z. 75: *to make an effort:* sich anstrengen, sich bemühen
Z. 76: *deceased:* verstorben
Z. 83 f.: *to support:* unterstützen
Z. 84: *confidence:* Zuversicht
Z. 87: *to achieve:* erreichen
Z. 89: *to focus on sth:* sich auf etwas konzentrieren

Aufgabe 1

✏ **Hinweis:** *Entscheide, ob die Aussagen richtig (True/T) oder falsch (False/F) sind bzw. ob es dazu im Text keine Informationen gibt (Not in the text/N).*

		T	F	N
a)	Kelechi plays for the national football team of Nigeria and played for the first team of Manchester City.	✓		
b)	Kelechi never had any doubts that he would make it to the top.		✓	
c)	Besides a Nigerian passport, Kelechi also has a British passport. ✏ **Hinweis:** *Es wird nicht erwähnt, welchen Pass Kelechi hat.*			✓
d)	Kelechi still has family in Nigeria.	✓		
e)	It was Kelechi's dream to become team captain of Manchester City one day.			✓
f)	Kelechi lives together with his father.		✓	

Aufgabe 2

✏ **Hinweis:** *Bringe die Fakten in die zeitlich richtige Reihenfolge. Der überzählige Satz passt inhaltlich nicht zum Lesetext.*

1. e
   ✏ Hinweis: *Z. 56 ff.*
2. d
   ✏ Hinweis: *Z. 34 f.*
3. f
   ✏ Hinweis: *Z. 20 ff.*
4. c
   ✏ Hinweis: *Z. 17 ff.*

Aufgabe 3

✏ **Hinweis:** *Beantworte die Fragen auf Grundlage des Lesetextes. Schreibe keine langen Sätze aus dem Text ab, sondern beschränke dich auf kurze (Teil-)Sätze bzw. Stichpunkte.*

a) (in) Nigeria
   ✏ Hinweis: *33 ff.*
b) Most Promising Talent of the Year
   ✏ Hinweis: *45 f.*
c) 18 (years old)
   ✏ Hinweis: *47 ff.*
d) 3/three (two brothers and one sister)
   ✏ Hinweis: *72 ff.*
e) to be/become a great player
   ✏ Hinweis: *91 f.*

Aufgabe 4

✏ **Hinweis:** *Finde die Stellen im Lesetext, die inhaltlich mit den Aussagen übereinstimmen. Notiere anschließend die Fundstellen durch Angabe der jeweiligen Zeilen.*

a) lines 30–32
b) lines 51–53
c) lines 66–69
d) lines 83/84
e) lines 92/93

Übungsaufgaben
Lösungen zum Kompetenzbereich „Text Production"

🖋 **Allgemeiner Hinweis:** *Für das gesamte Kapitel „Text Production" ist es wichtig, dass du dir die Arbeitsschritte zum Verfassen eines Textes im Trainingsband auf Seite 37 f. genau durchliest und dementsprechend arbeitest. Wenn du nach diesen Schritten vorgehst, wird dir ein gut strukturierter Text bestimmt nicht mehr schwerfallen. Die folgenden Lösungen sind Beispiele, an denen du dich orientieren kannst.*

Aufgabe 1

🖋 **Hinweis:** *Hier musst du noch keinen vollständigen Text schreiben, sondern einen vorgegebenen Satz abändern. Du kannst dabei üben, Sätze sprachlich zu variieren.*

a) I like **our house**, which **is old / is at the end of the street**.
b) At the end of **the street** you find **our (old) house**.
c) The street ends where **our (old) house is**.
d) Do you know the house **at the end of the street**? It's **our house/ours/old**.
e) Our **house** is **old** and **at the end of the street**.

Aufgabe 2

🖋 **Hinweis:** *Konjunktionen helfen dir, Sätze elegant zu verknüpfen und diese nicht nur aneinanderzureihen. Es ist hilfreich, wenn du sie mit Beispielsätzen in deine Vokabelkartei aufnimmst. Zur den deutschen Entsprechungen der englischen Konjunktionen vergleiche die Kurzgrammatik auf S. 78 f.*

a) **After / When** I left the house this morning I noticed that I had left behind my umbrella.
b) I would have needed it **because** it started to rain.
c) **As** I did not want to get wet I took the bus.
d) **When** I got off the bus, it was still raining.
e) It rained so heavily **that** I got completely wet.
f) **Although** I drank a cup of hot tea in the office, I was ill the next day **and** had to stay in bed.

Aufgabe 3

✏ Hinweis: Die Teilaufgaben a) und b) helfen dir dabei, Ideen und einen treffenden Wortschatz für deine Geschichte zusammenzustellen. Die in der Beispiellösung verwendeten Ideen und Wörter sind unterstrichen. Gestalte den Hauptteil der Geschichte – also den Teil, in dem etwas Überraschendes passieren soll – mit wörtlicher Rede aus.

c) *Beispiellösung:*
One Saturday afternoon, Lisa was in town to do some shopping. In front of some street cafés, she saw an artist juggling with clubs. "He is really good", Lisa thought and stopped to watch. Three friends, Chynna, Nick and Dave, joined to watch.
Suddenly, a man ran towards them. "Out of the way!" he yelled and pulled Lisa's handbag off her shoulder with such force that she fell to the ground. Nick and Dave started to chase the thief, while Chynna helped Lisa back to her feet. "All my belongings are inside my bag!" she cried. Nick and Dave returned with bad news: "We saw the guy escape in a car." "And where did the juggler go?" Lisa asked, and everybody realised that he had left.
The next day, the police found Lisa's empty bag in a bin. One of the policemen explained that the juggler and the thief were a wanted pair of criminals and this was their favourite trick.
(161 words)

Aufgabe 4

✏ **Hinweis:** Die Aufgabenstellung enthält ein Bild mit Stichwörtern, auf deren Grundlage du eine Geschichte schreiben sollst. Betrachte zuerst das Bild: zwei junge Leute trampen, der Zeitraum ist vorgegeben („Last August..."). Überlege in einem zweiten Schritt, welchen (Reise-)plan die jungen Leute wohl haben. Welches unerwartete Ereignis könnte eintreten und wie fühlen sich die einzelnen Personen dabei? Im nächsten Schritt wählst du deine besten Ideen aus. Welche Ideen kannst du der Einleitung, dem Hauptteil und dem Schluss zuordnen? Verbinde deine Sätze mit Konjunktionen (z. B. „and", „because", „while"). Schreibe in der Zeitform „Simple past" (z. B. was/were, wanted...). Verwende auch die wörtliche Rede, um deine Geschichte lebendiger zu machen.

a) *Beispiellösung Notizen:*
   Reiseziel, Pläne:
   - hitchhike to a music festival in Italy
   - not enough money for the trip: work and travel:
     Jessica: waitress in a café

Jesse: plays the guitar in the pedestrian zone
Unerwartetes Ereignis, Gefühle:
- Jessica meets an Italian guy in the café
- Jesse is angry

b) *Beispiellösung Geschichte:*

Summer trip

Last August, Jessica and her older brother Jesse were on their way to a music festival in Italy. They did not have enough money to pay for the trip so they decided to hitchhike. They were lucky because some friendly drivers gave them a lift.

After arriving at the small Italian town at the coast Jessica soon found a job as a waitress at a café. Jesse played his guitar in the pedestrian zone, but he was not very successful. When the music festival started, a good-looking guest said to Jessica: "Hi, my name is Alberto. Would you like to go to the festival with me?" "What a cute guy!" thought Jessica. At the festival, Jessica and Alberto were flirting all the time, while Jesse was sitting next to them feeling alone and depressed. His sister was having a good time and he didn't even have enough money to buy himself a drink! "That is certainly not my idea of a great holiday!" Jesse thought angrily.

(166 words)

Aufgabe 5

Hinweis: *Wie bei Aufgabe 4 wird dir ein Bild vorgegeben, bei dem zwei junge Leute per Anhalter unterwegs sind. Diesmal ist das Thema durch das Bild und die Vorgaben stärker eingegrenzt. Bei näherer Betrachtung der Zeichnung erfährst du zum einen, wohin die Fahrt gehen soll, nämlich nach Dublin, die Hauptstadt von Irland. Zum anderen trägt der junge Mann einen ausgefallenen Hut, der aufgrund seiner Form und des „Shamrocks" (Kleeblatt) auf die Feiern zum St. Patrick's Day hinweist. Die Wortvorgabe „Pleiten, Pech und Pannen" weist darauf hin, dass während des Trips das ein oder andere schiefgeht.*

Beispiellösung Notizen:

Anreise:

- Tina and Tom: hitchhiking to Dublin, it starts to rain
- bus stops: tour bus with musicians, singing and music during the trip

Pleiten, Pech und Pannen:

- forgot their backpack at the side of the road

Erlebnisse, Pleiten, Pech und Pannen:

- Dublin full of tourists, hotels fully booked

- train back home the same evening

Rückkehr:
- watch the St. Patrick's Day parade on TV the next day

Beispiellösung Geschichte:

A trip to remember

The day before St. Patrick's Day, Tina and Tom wanted to hitchhike to Dublin. While they were waiting at side of the road, it started to rain and they didn't have an umbrella with them. Unfortunately, no cars went past, but suddenly a bus stopped nearby. Inside was a cheerful band that was also going to Dublin to play in the parade the next day. "Welcome aboard!" said the band leader. After an hour of music and singing, they arrived in Dublin. That was when Tina and Tom realised that they had left their backpack at the side of the road, so Tina phoned home: "Mum, could you please get our backpack?" Her mother wasn't happy about that. Luckily, they had their money and valuables *(Wertsachen)* with them. In the next few hours they looked for a hotel room. "Sorry, we're fully booked" was what all the receptionists said. With no place to sleep, Tina and Tom decided to take the night train back home. The next day the two unlucky friends watched the St. Patrick's Day parade on TV. *(180 words)*

Aufgabe 6

✏ **Hinweis:** *In den vorgegeben Bildern wird eine kurze Geschichte erzählt. Fasse sie in Worte und finde einen passenden und interessanten Schluss. Die Bildergeschichte lässt dir viel Raum für eigene Ideen, da das Ende offen ist. Du kannst folgendermaßen vorgehen:*

Schritt 1: Betrachtung der Bilder: ein junger Mann (Luke) geht im Park spazieren und schaut auf sein Handy, da er eine Textnachricht erhalten hat; vor seinen Füßen liegt eine Bananenschale.

Schritt 2: Brainstorming: Von wem könnte die Nachricht stammen? Welchen Inhalt hat die Nachricht? Hat die Bananenschale irgendwelche Folgen für Luke (z. B. Sturz)?

Schritt 3: Verfassen des Textes: Bringe deine Ideen als zusammenhängende Geschichte zu Papier. Schreibe im „Simple past" (z. B. receiv<u>ed</u>). Verwende auch die wörtliche Rede, um deine Geschichte lebendiger zu machen.

Beispiellösung:

A banana in the way

Luke was taking a walk in the park when he received a message from his brother Dave: "Sarah and I are getting married!" Luke smiled and wrote back: "Wow, that's great! When is the wedding?"
While he was looking at his mobile, Luke stepped on a banana peel on the path, slipped, almost fell to the ground and dropped his mobile. He heard the display crash and the mobile went out.
"That phone was new!" Luke moaned.
"Looks like this is not your lucky day," a young woman said smiling as she came towards him from the opposite direction.
"No, it's not." Luke replied. "My brother wanted to tell me about his wedding, but now my mobile is broken."
"I could lend you mine if you want to call him back." the woman said and handed him her phone. Luke was surprised but took it and smiled at her. He then noticed that the woman looked quite nice.
After Luke had made his call, he asked the woman if he could invite her for a coffee – and she said yes! In the end, the day turned into a lucky one for Luke!

(177 words)

Aufgabe 7

Hinweis: *Eine Bildergeschichte wie diese findest du häufig in der Abschlussprüfung. Betrachte in einem ersten Schritt die Bilder: die Keksdose ist leer, der Mann ist wütend, er schimpft die Katze, die Frau serviert die Kekse auf einem Tablett, der Mann bringt der Katze einen Kuchen. Verfasse nun deinen Text. Der Hauptteil, in dem der Mann zunächst die Katze verdächtigt und beschimpft, bis er herausfindet, dass er seinem Haustier Unrecht getan hat, sollte besonders ausgestaltet werden. Verwende dabei auch die wörtliche Rede sowie passende Adjektive und Adverbien.*

The suspect

Mr Smith wanted to have some biscuits at teatime. He looked into the biscuit box – but it was empty! Mr Smith grabbed his cat Kitty by the neck and showed her the empty box. He shouted: "You've eaten my biscuits!" Angrily, Mr Smith went to the kitchen to tell his wife that the biscuits were gone. Mrs Smith was preparing some tea and biscuits. Now he realised that his wife had emptied the biscuit box and not their cat! This made Mr Smith feel guilty, so he apologised to the cat for his bad behaviour by giving her a very yummy cake.

(102 words)

Aufgabe 8

Hinweis: Betrachte auch bei dieser Bildergeschichte zuerst die einzelnen Bilder und versuche, zu verstehen, was passiert: Junge Frau (Jenny) steigt in Zug, erhält während der Fahrt Textnachricht auf dem Smartphone, Freunde machen am Bahnsteig auf sich aufmerksam, Jenny verpasst die Haltestelle, sie sitzt an der nächsten Haltestelle und denkt daran, was die Freunde jetzt wohl machen. In deinem Text solltest du besonders auf Bild 4 eingehen, da es entscheidend für das Verständnis der Geschichte ist und den Höhepunkt ausmacht. Verwende in deiner Geschichte auch die wörtliche Rede. Der folgende Text ist eine Beispiellösung.

One stop too far

On Saturday evening, Jenny got on the train to meet her friends at a party. She found a nice window seat, and started to use her smartphone. She wrote to her friends: "Meet you at 6 pm at Oldham Station. Looking forward to the party :-)" Then she switched to a game app. Jenny was so busy playing her game that she didn't notice the train arriving at Oldham Station. She also didn't see her friends, who came to meet her at the station and who were waving and shouting to catch her attention: "Jenny, get off the train!"; but Jenny was so concentrated on her game that she didn't see them.

It was 8 pm when Jenny sat on a bench at Weston Station. She was very unhappy that she had missed Oldham Station and now had to wait for the next train to take her back to Oldham. She thought of her friends, having a lot of fun at the party now, and she didn't look at her smartphone again that evening.

(174 words)

Aufgabe 9

Hinweis: Diese Vorübung im Stil eines Austausches von Textnachrichten verlangt, dass du dich sowohl mit den Aussagen deiner englischsprachigen Chatpartnerin Jessy befasst, als auch auf die deutschen Vorgaben eingehst. Der Stil ist umgangssprachlich, d.h., Abkürzungen, die im Chat üblich sind, dürfen verwendet werden, z. B. TGIF (Thank God it's Friday).

Jessy: Hi! I'm sorry for writing late. I'm just on my way to school. TGIF! How was your day?

Du: My school day was OK. In the morning I had a test in English, which went well. I'm having a late lunch now and I'm going to meet my friends at the shopping mall later.

Jessy: You're sooo lucky that you're already done with school for this week! My friend's having a sleepover party at her house tonight. Not sure if I'll go though. I don't feel well. What are your plans for the weekend?

Du: **My family is invited to my aunt's wedding on Sunday. I need a new dress for it, so that's why I'm going to the mall later.**

Jessy: Sounds great! You know, it's going to be so much fun once you come over to stay with us! By the way, my mom wants to know if there is any food that you don't like???

Du: **Thank your mom for asking! Honestly, I don't really like meat. I prefer vegetables and milk products. My mom showed me how to make a really great dish with potatoes, vegetables and cheese in the oven. If you like, I could show you how to make this when I am in Canada.**

Jessy: Sounds yummy! Anything else you'd like to know?

Du: **When I stay with your family, am I going to have my own room or am I going to share it with you? Do you think I could also go to a language course? I really want to improve my English.
Is there a pool close to your house? I love swimming!
As a present for your parents I could bring some of my aunt's home-made honey. Do you think they would like that?**

Jessy: Sorry! Have to get back to you later on all of that. We just arrived at school. Bye!

Aufgabe 10

🖉 Hinweis: *Bei dieser Vorübung zur Aufgabenvariante „Correspondence" ist die Struktur der Postkarte bereits durch Satzanfänge vorgegeben. Dies erleichtert dir das Schreiben. Beim Vervollständigen der Postkarte solltest du darauf achten, auf die deutschen Vorgaben einzugehen.*

3 January 20xx

Dear (aunt) Emily,

Best **wishes** from Johannesburg! I'm here with **mum and dad**. This place is **fantastic/great**! The weather is **hot and sunny** and I'm feeling **good/fantastic/great/wonderful/a bit tired because of the heat/ …**
This is what we've already done in our holidays:
After arriving in Cape Town we spent a couple of days at a hotel at the beach. We also went sightseeing and shopping in the city, but the best part was the hike up to Lion's Head. We had a great view of the city and the ocean from there. On our last day in Cape Town Dad and I also did a surf course at False Bay and I was much better than him!

And we have further plans:
Tomorrow, we're going on a trip to Kruger National Park where we'll stay at a lodge. The day after we're going on a safari in the park. I really hope we'll see some big animals before we fly back home!
Love,
(your name)

Aufgabe 11

🖉 **Hinweis:** *Diese Aufgabe ist einer Aufgabe in der Prüfung schon recht ähnlich. Du bekommst eine E-Mail auf Englisch vorgelegt sowie zusätzliche Vorgaben auf Deutsch, die in deiner Antwort-Mail zu berücksichtigen sind. Lies zuerst, was Sean geschrieben hat, und kläre ggf. unbekannten Wortschatz, z. B. „to look for" = „suchen nach", „to wonder" = „sich fragen", „application" = „Bewerbung". Befasse dich dann mit den Vorgaben, die beim Erstellen der E-Mail aufzugreifen sind. Gehe sie der Reihe nach durch und schreibe zu jeder Vorgabe einen oder mehrere passende englische Sätze. Falls deine E-Mail dann noch nicht den nötigen Umfang hat, solltest du deinen Text entsprechend den Vorgaben weiter ausarbeiten oder eigene, passende Ideen einbringen (z. B. einen weiteren Vorschlag für eine gemeinsame Unternehmung). Die folgende E-Mail ist eine Beispiellösung.*

Hi Sean,

How are you? Thank you for your e-mail. I'm happy because I got a job at a hotel in Cambridge for the holidays. That's great, isn't it? I'll have to clean the rooms or support the staff at the reception, or help out in the kitchen. I'm glad that I'll earn some money. Afterwards I'll still have one week of my holidays left and I would love to spend it in Dublin with you. It would be a pity if I only worked during my holidays! I'd really like to come in the last week of August and I'm looking forward to the festival you told me about.

Take care,

(your name)   *(113 words)*

Aufgabe 12

🖉 **Hinweis:** *Bei dieser „Correspondence"-Aufgabe bekommst du abgesehen von der englischen E-Mail keine weiteren inhaltlichen Vorgaben. Lies die Aufgabenstellung sowie die vorgegebene E-Mail zuerst sorgfältig durch. In der Prüfung kannst du unbekannte Wörter ggf. im Wörterbuch nachschlagen, z. B. „to guess" = „raten", „wildlife rescue station" = „Auffangstation für Wildtiere", „to drop somebody off" = „je-*

manden absetzen", „possum" = kleines australisches Beuteltier, „something matters"
= „etwas ist wichtig/macht einen Unterschied".
Beim Schreiben hast du relativ große Freiheit. Stelle jedoch stets einen Bezug zu
Vanessas E-Mail her. Gehe z. B. auf ihren Wunsch ein, dir einmal alle Tiere zeigen zu
können, und antworte auf ihre Fragen. Die folgende E-Mail ist eine Beispiellösung.

Dear Vanessa,

Thanks for your e-mail! You're so lucky that it's hot in Australia. It's freezing here in Germany and it has already snowed a little bit! My holidays are fine, but I have a cold …
It sounds like you're having a wonderful internship at the wildlife rescue station. I would also like to do that. I think it's great that you help injured animals. Do they bite you sometimes? I hope not. Where did you find the baby camel? And how big is a baby camel?
I would also be happy if you could show the station and the animals to me someday. I've already asked my mom if I could get a trip to Australia for Christmas. She said it's too expensive, but I'm saving some money and maybe I'll be able to visit you in a year!

Take care,
(your name) (143 words)

Aufgabe 13 a

✏ **Hinweis:** *Die Aufgaben 13 a und 13 b sind gelenkte Vorübungen zu Aufgabe 14. Die Angaben aus der Stellenanzeige sowie aus dem Bewerbungsformular (13 a) helfen dir, die Sätze im Bewerbungsschreiben (13 b) sinnvoll zu ergänzen. In der Prüfung musst du dann in der Lage sein, ein Bewerbungsschreiben auch ohne die oben genannten Hilfen zu verfassen. Lerne dazu den Aufbau eines Bewerbungsschreibens sowie typische Redewendungen (siehe 13 b) auswendig.*

Beispiellösung:

Name: __Thomas__ (first) __Bauer__ (last)
Gender: ☐ female ☒ male ☐ other
Date of birth: __7/8/20xx__
Nationality: __German__
E-Mail: __th.bauer@online.de__

Position you want to apply for:
☒ receptionist ☐ room service ☐ kitchen help

Availability:
From: __1st__ (day) __July__ (month) __20XX__ (year)
To: __31st__ (day) __August__ (month) __20XX__ (year)

How many hours do you want to work per week?
☐ under 10 ☐ 10–20 ☒ 20–30 ☐ over 30

Preferred working period: ☒ mornings ☐ afternoons ☐ evenings

Do you have a valid driver's licence? ☐ yes ☒ no

Languages spoken: ☒ English ☐ French ☐ Spanish
☒ Others: __German__

Current occupation: ☒ student ☐ apprentice ☐ employed ☐ unemployed

Work experience:
__internship in a small hotel__

What makes you a true Oceanview Hotel staff member? I am …
☒ hard-working ☐ open-minded ☒ friendly ☐ helpful
☐ independent ☐ flexible ☒ ready to learn ☐ reliable
☐ skilful ☐ clever ☒ communicative ☐ sociable

Aufgabe 13 b

Hinweis: Lies dir den Einleitungstext und die Anzeige genau durch. Die Angaben in der Anzeige helfen dir, die Sätze sinnvoll zu ergänzen. Du kannst dir als Hilfe für deine Ergänzungen auch noch einmal das Bewerbungsformular ansehen.

Dear Mr Leary,

I saw your job advert **on the internet** and I am interested in working at **Oceanview Hotel as a receptionist**. My name is …, I am … years old and I live in …, Germany.

I am graduating from school in **June**. I have been learning English for **five** years and can speak it **well**. During my last summer holidays I **did an internship at a small hotel in my hometown**.

I am the right person for the job because **I am friendly and communicative**. Working at your hotel would be a great opportunity for me to **gain some more experience**.
Could you please give me some more information about the job?
How long **would I have to work every day**? How much **do you pay**?
I look forward **to hearing from you**.

Yours sincerely,

(your name)

Aufgabe 14 a

✎ Hinweis: Die Aufgaben 14a und 14b erfordern ein Bewerbungsschreiben bzw. einen Lebenslauf (CV) in Tabellenform. Wenn dir das Verfassen eines Bewerbungsschreibens noch schwerfällt, bearbeite zunächst die Aufgaben 13a und 13b. Die folgende Lösung ist eine Beispiellösung.

Dear Mrs Jackson,

I would like to apply for a job as a waiter/waitress at the River Café. My agency "Trips Down Under" suggested that I contact you.

I am 18 years old and I am soon going to finish my apprenticeship as a retail salesman/saleswoman at a department store. Before I start my first job I would like to gain some experience abroad and improve my English.

I am interested in the position of waiter/waitress because I enjoy working in service with customers and I also like working in a team.

I could start in November and stay for three months.

Finally, I would like to ask you how long I would have to work each day and how much I would earn.

I look forward to your reply.

Yours sincerely,

(your name)

Aufgabe 14 b

✎ **Hinweis:** *Der folgende Lebenslauf ist ein Beispiel, an dem du dich orientieren kannst. Hier findest du auch typische Begriffe, die in einem Lebenslauf verwendet werden.*

CV

Personal information	Surname/Family name: Huber First name: Alexander Date of birth: 10 January 20xx Place of birth: Fürth/Germany
Education	• Middle school certificate • Apprentice as a retail salesman at Quick-Kauf department store in Erlangen
Practical experience	Summer job as a waiter at Schlossgarten Café, Erlangen (3 weeks)
Skills	Casual conversation with customers in English
Personal interests	Sports (basketball, volleyball, running) Dogs

> **Übungsaufgaben**
> **Lösungen zum Kompetenzbereich „Speaking"**

✏ **Allgemeiner Hinweis:** *Du findest hier Aufgaben zu allen Bereichen der mündlichen Prüfung. Lies die Aufgabenstellungen genau durch, aber beachte, dass du sie in der Prüfung nicht vorgelegt bekommst, und die Aufgaben und Fragen ausschließlich mündlich an dich gerichtet werden. Beantworte alle Punkte möglichst ausführlich und begründe deine Antworten.*

Aufgabe 1

✏ **Hinweis:** *Du hast hier 30 Sekunden Zeit, um das Foto zu betrachten und dir einen Überblick zu verschaffen, was auf dem Bild zu sehen ist. Achte auch schon auf Details (Wie viele Personen? Was ist zu sehen? Welche Situation? Etc.). Zunächst werden dir konkrete Fragen zum Bild gestellt, danach weiterführende Fragen. Versuche umfassend und logisch zu antworten. Du kannst natürlich jederzeit einen Blick auf das Bild werfen, um die gewünschten Informationen abzurufen.*

Beispiellösung:

a) I see a room. It is probably a music studio because a band is performing there, and it doesn't look like they're on a stage. The wall is white and has little holes in it. There is a window that looks out onto another room. I also see a long dark curtain. On the floor there might be a carpet.

b) There are four people – two young men and two young women – making music. The young man on the left is playing the keyboard. He is looking directly at the camera. The woman in the centre has her eyes closed while she is singing into the microphone. The guy on the right is playing an electric guitar. The girl at the back of the photo has raised her arms. She looks like she is about to strike the percussion instrument she is playing. Each of the musicians is smiling as they play their instruments.

c) All the musicians are wearing casual clothes. The two men are dressed in a similar way, and so are the two women. The guy with the guitar is wearing jeans and an undershirt, the other boy a T-shirt. The woman in the front is wearing torn dark trousers, a white T-shirt and a checked shirt. The drummer's shirt is the same style as the singer's.

d) I think it's more fun to make music when you're in a group. Doing something in a team is generally more fun than doing something on your own. As there are several instruments, the music becomes more interesting, too. Playing in a group is also a way to improve by learning from each other.

e) I like listening to pop music on the radio. My favourite station has a great mix of the latest hits in the morning. Listening to it helps start the day with energy.

Aufgabe 2

Hinweis: Was fällt dir auf dem Foto auf? Warum könnte der Mann verkleidet sein und was hält er in seinen Händen? Wie deutest du den Gesichtsausdruck der Frau?

Beispiellösung:

a) The man is standing in a pedestrian zone and is wearing a funny costume. He's holding some flyers in his hands. The woman is passing by and looking at him in a surprised way.

b) The man is dressed up as a chicken head to toe. Only his face and hands are showing. His face is looking out of the chicken's beak. The upper part of his body is covered with a material that looks like feathers. His legs and feet are covered by a smooth cloth. His feet look like bird's claws.
The woman is wearing a skirt, a blouse and a short cardigan. She also has a pair of glasses on her head and a handbag hanging from her shoulder.

c) The weather seems to be sunny and warm, but not too hot. The people in the picture are casting shadows on the ground and the woman has a pair of sunglasses on her head. There are also some parasols in the background and some people are sitting outdoors at the café.

d) The man is wearing the chicken costume to draw people's attention. He might work for a store or a company for whom he does advertising. I think the papers in his hands are flyers informing people about an event or special offer at a store nearby; but he could also work for an animal protection organization, trying to inform people about the bad living conditions of chicken on chicken farms.

e) Sometimes there are street artists in the city centre. Most of the time I don't stop to watch them. There are, for instance, these men in suits and hats that are painted completely in gold or silver and who stand still like statues. They are not my favourite ones. I like street musicians much better. Some of them are really good artists. If I like their music and I'm not in a rush, I stop and throw some coins into their hats.

Aufgabe 3

Hinweis: *Betrachte das Foto. Wie alt sind die dargestellten Personen ungefähr und welche Beziehung könnten sie zueinander haben? An welchem Ort könnte das Bild aufgenommen worden sein? Womit befassen die Jugendlichen sich gerade?*

Beispiellösung:

a) The four teenagers are outdoors. They're sitting on the ground and leaning against a low wall. In the background, there are the chairs of a café or restaurant. I think the young people are in a public place like a pedestrian zone.

b) Each of the teenagers has a smartphone in their hands. There's also a skateboard, which probably belongs to one of the boys. Next to each girl there is a bag.

c) It doesn't look like they are communicating with each other. Instead they are busy with their smartphones all by themselves. Maybe they are communicating with other people, writing messages to them, or they are using apps or playing games.

d) Yes, it looks like the four young people are good friends. They are sitting close to each other on the pavement. The arms of the boy and girl in the middle are touching, and the boy in the middle has also put his arm behind the boy on the right. They also have a similar style of clothing (leather jackets and denim jeans, for example), which is often typical of good friends.

e) Both things are important: Meeting friends personally and staying in contact with them via messages or social networks. When I meet my friends, we can talk face to face, make jokes, laugh and have a lot of fun together. I can look at my friends' faces and see how they are feeling, or give them a hug when they are sad or worried. It is not possible to have the same kind of experience when your friends are not around in person. But I also don't want to do without staying in touch with my friends online. The advantage is that we can communicate even if we are far apart from each other or if we're busy with other things. It can also be fun to text each other and make jokes that way, or to send each other selfies of where we are at the moment.

Aufgabe 4

Hinweis: *Sieh dir den Werbespot an. Welche Personen kommen vor? Mit welchem Problem wird der Mann konfrontiert? Wie löst er das Problem? Ist der Spot ernst oder humorvoll? An welche Zielgruppe könnte er sich richten? Wozu wird der Zuschauer (indirekt) aufgefordert?*

Beispiellösung:

Scene description: In the video you see a father carrying his little daughter to the car. When they have almost reached the car, the girl shows her father that her doll has lost a shoe. This makes the father go back over the hot sand to pick it up.

a) He desperately wants to reach his car because he is walking barefoot on hot sand and carrying his daughter as well as lots of beach equipment. He is suffering because of his heavy load, and because the hot sand and the pebbles on the car park make his feet hurt.

b) The doll has lost its shoe on the way from the beach to the car. It is now lying somewhere in the hot sand.

c) The father is unhappy because he realizes that he will have to go back to fetch the shoe, but when his daughter looks at him hopefully, he knows he has got to go back.

d) Yes, the father behaves like a superhero because first he has to walk on the hot sand to take his daughter and the beach equipment to the parking lot, and then he turns around again to go back to fetch the doll's shoe. He also doesn't leave his daughter by the car but takes her with him to get the shoe. When he turns around to go down the beach again, the wind blows up the beach towel that is wrapped around his neck, making it look like the cape of a superhero.

e) The message behind the car being "for real superheros" probably refers to parents who would do anything for their family and children. These parents are the ones who deserve this car, which is only for special people. While a superhero from a comic is a fictional character with supernatural powers (e.g. Batman, Spiderman, etc.) a "real" superhero according to this video clip is the ordinary, loving father, who does everything for his child.

Aufgabe 5

🖉 **Hinweis:** *Hier findest du eine Beispiellösung zu jedem der 6 Aspekte. Wie in der Aufgabe beschrieben, sprichst du nur zu 3 Stichpunkten. In der Prüfung ist es genauso richtig, z. B. ganz allgemein über das Leben in kanadischen Städten zu sprechen oder aber Faktenwissen zu ausgewählten Städten zu nennen. Vergiss nicht, deinem Vortrag eine Struktur zu geben, z. B.: "My topic is …" / "The aspects I have chosen are …" / "I'll start with … (because…)"*

Beispiellösung:

I'm going to tell you something about Canada. My first aspect is "**landscape**". Canada is the 2nd largest country in the world and it has a lot of different landscapes: the Atlantic and Pacific Coast, the Rocky Mountains, the Great Lakes, the prairies and the Arctic regions. Besides, Canada has many islands, such as Vancouver Island and Newfoundland.

Now I'd like to talk about Canadian **cities**. Although Canada is a very big country, it only has less than half as many inhabitants as Germany. As a result, you don't find many big cities there. The capital is Ottawa. Other major cities are Montreal, Quebec, Toronto and Vancouver. The oldest cities are in the very south of the country because it's warmer there, while new cities like Calgary and Edmonton in the Rockies lie further north. In a city you can reach school, your workplace or a hospital quite comfortably, even if there's a lot of snow and ice. This is much harder or even impossible if you live in a remote area.

As my third aspect I've chosen "**native population**". Canada's native population consists of the First Nations and the Inuit, who mostly live in their own communities. The Inuit, for example, have claimed their own territory, Nunavut, in the far north of Canada. In the course of history, all native peoples have been victims to the expansion of the European colonists, who came primarily from England and France. Today the government has made some efforts to support the indigenous population, but many native communities still face problems like poverty, bad housing and alcoholism. I think the way the native peoples used to live was better than the European way. They lived mostly in harmony with nature and only took what they needed for living – and they never caused environmental problems like modern society does. I think life in a tribe was similar to life in a big family. People took care of one another. I think people were happier then.

The main **languages** in Canada are English and French. These languages were brought to Canada by British and French settlers. Today English and French are both official languages. About 20% of Canadians speak French as their mother tongue. It is mainly spoken in Quebec. There are also the languages of the indigenous tribes such as the First Nations and the arctic tribes in the north. I think it is great that you can speak English in Canada. As English is a world language it makes it easy for people from all over the world to go to Canada and communicate easily while they are there.

If you think of Canada, **animals** like wolves, grizzly bears, moose and polar bears come to mind. I like polar bears most, especially the white colour of their fur, and I think it is great that they are able to survive in the Arctic. I once saw a film about polar bear watching, which has become a tourist attraction in Canada, but I've also learned that they are threatened by extinction because of climate change. As their hunting areas are getting smaller, polar bears are more likely to approach human settlements in search of food. By doing this, they are becoming a problem to peo-

ple. I hope that Canada's government will do its best to protect these amazing animals.
My last point is about Canadian **tourist attractions**. I think that the Niagara Falls are one of the biggest tourist attractions there. It must be very impressive to watch the water fall down hundreds of metres and I'd like to see that myself one day. Canada is also famous for winter sports. You can do all kinds of sports that have to do with ice and snow, such as skiing, ice-skating or going for a ride with a dog-sled. Tourists who love nature and wildlife are attracted by Canada as well. You can go hiking, join a guided tour with a ranger or go on a whale watching tour. Tourists are also attracted by cities like Quebec with its French colonial flair, or Calgary, where a famous rodeo event takes place every year.

Aufgabe 6

🖉 **Hinweis:** *Du findest hier eine Beispiellösung zu allen sechs Aspekten. In der Prüfung sprichst du nur zu drei Stichwörtern.*
Beispiellösung „Topic-based talk":
I'd like to give a little talk about the topic "holidays". My first keyword is holiday **destinations**. In summertime, many people want to leave their homes and travel. Typical destinations are the sea, the mountains or interesting cities. Most people like to travel with their families or in groups to have a better experience. Those who go to the sea typically lie on the beach, spending long hours in the sun. Beach holidays are the most popular holiday choice with children. Others prefer the mountains and the many possibilities of physical exercise that they offer, such as hiking, mountain biking, rock climbing or skiing in the winter. I'm dreaming of spending a holiday with my best friends at a resort in Florida.
My second point is **transport**, so it's about how you can reach your holiday destination. The classic way of travelling is by car. This is the easiest way to transport one's belongings to the holiday location, but in order to reach distant places, most travellers also take a plane. While travelling by train is a popular option for city tours, other tourists like to go on holiday on ship cruises.
Now I'd like to give some information about holiday **seasons**. You can go on a holiday all year round, but the season you want to go on holiday depends on what you want to do during your vacation. A lot of people like to go on holiday in summer, but it is not the only time of the year that's great for vacations. Lovers of winter sports wait all year until it finally gets cold. The Alps, for example are great for skiing, snowboarding and sledding. City tours, for example to Paris and New York, are usually best in spring and autumn when it's neither too hot nor too cold.

What do **languages** have to do with holidays? Well, if you don't stay in your home country, you have to be prepared to communicate with people who speak another language. Tourists usually get along with English all over the world. In most western countries, English is spoken by many people, especially by service personnel in hotels or holiday resorts. The adventurous travel to exotic places where communication can be a challenge. Still the experience can be great.

Finally, I want to talk about **problems** while you are on holiday. Many things can go wrong during a holiday trip. Getting ill is typically the most frequent and annoying thing. Sometimes the problems start before you have reached your holiday resort – you can miss a plane, your car can break down or you realise that your passport isn't valid any more. Depending on where you're heading, local crime can also be an issue.

An important aspect is **cultural differences**, which sometimes need getting used to, like dress codes for women in Arabic countries. Therefore it is good to be well-informed about local customs before going on holiday.

Beispiellösung „Oral report", Thema „Holidays":

*⁂ **Hinweis:** Hier bekommst du keine Stichwörter in Form einer Mindmap vorgelegt, sondern du musst selbst überlegen, was du zum Thema „Holidays" sagen könntest. Notiere dir aber Stichwörter und übe das freie Sprechen.*
Denke daran, dein Referat klar zu gliedern:
Einleitung: *Nenne das Thema deines Referats und begründe, warum du es gewählt hast.*
Hauptteil: *Wenn du über einen Urlaub berichtest, kannst du der Reihe nach erzählen, was passiert ist, oder du suchst dir nur bestimmte wichtige Ereignisse aus, von denen du berichtest. Wenn du Fachbegriffe verwendest, oder die Namen bestimmter Attraktionen nennst, solltest du erklären, was sie bedeuten, bzw. was es dort zu sehen gibt. Bringe zur Veranschaulichung Fotos oder Souvenirs mit oder erstelle ein Plakat.*
Schluss: *Fasse den Inhalt deines Referats kurz zusammen oder finde einen Schluss, der das Referat abrundet.*
In der Prüfung könnten folgende Fragen gestellt werden: "What activity did you like best and why? What sights did you see? What was your best memory?"

I would like to tell you about the fantastic holiday I spent with my family this summer. My parents, my sister and I stayed three weeks in Florida, which is a very exciting place to go to.

In the middle of August, we flew to Miami. As we had to change planes in Chicago, the trip took 15 hours and we were very tired when we arrived. My parents rented a car at the airport and we drove to a holiday flat in Fort Lauderdale, where we all fell into bed. The next day, we all wanted to go to the beach first, so we drove to Miami Beach where we had a beach picnic for lunch. It was 36 to 38 degrees and you had to wear sandals when walking in the sand because it was so hot! But my sister and I ran into the sea and it was great!

The first week we stayed in Fort Lauderdale. We went to the beach and sometimes went on a trip. In Miami we visited the Seaquarium, where they do shows with killer whales and dolphins. We also went to a parrot park, where we saw thousands of colourful birds. Some birds even sat down on the visitors and we took a lot of photos there. Once, we also went to a big flea market in Fort Lauderdale, where we stayed for the whole afternoon. My sister and I bought some souvenirs there.

In the second week, we first drove to Orlando, which is in the middle of Florida, where we stayed in a motel for a couple of days. We went to some fun parks like Disney World and the MGM Studios. But I liked the Epcot Center best. It is a big park where you can go on different rides but also see a lot of interesting films or shows about other cultures, nature or animals. The next time I go to Florida, I will go to the Epcot Center again for sure! After Orlando, we drove to the Lyndon B. Johnson Space Center, where we lost my sister and had to look for her for two hours before we found her. So we didn't see all of the spaceships. We then spent a few more days at the beach.

At the end of our holiday, my father wanted to go to Key West. We drove for a whole day, and at the end of the trip we crossed a lot of bridges which go right over the ocean. In Key West we went to the spot which is the southernmost tip of the USA. We bought more souvenirs and went to see a museum about treasure hunting in the sea. We also saw the house of Ernest Hemingway, the famous author.

We were all sad when we had to drive back to the airport in Miami, but my parents promised that we would travel to Florida again!

Aufgabe 7

Hinweis: *Übertrage vom Englischen ins Deutsche und umgekehrt. Du musst nicht zwangsläufig wortwörtlich übersetzen. Auch wenn in der Prüfung von dir nicht verlangt wird, einen Perspektivwechsel vorzunehmen, ist dieser hier zusätzlich angegeben.*

a) Guten Morgen. Was kann ich für Sie tun?
b) I have a problem with my foot. It really hurts. /
My grandma has a problem with her foot. ...
c) Wo tut es genau weh? Könnten Sie es mir zeigen? / Kannst du es ihr zeigen?
d) Down here. The skin is also red. / The skin has also turned red.
e) Hatten Sie dieses Problem schon einmal? /
Sie fragt, ob du dieses Problem schon einmal hattest.
f) I don't think so. It's new. / She doesn't think so. It's new.
g) Was ist mit Ihren Schuhen? Kratzt oder reibt der Schuh auf der Haut? /
Was ist mit deinen Schuhen? ...
h) No, they aren't. My/Her shoes are really comfortable.
i) Also ich denke, Sie sollten zum Arzt gehen. Nebenan gibt es einen sehr guten. Warum gehen Sie nicht dahin?/Gehen Sie doch dorthin. /
Sie schlägt vor, zum Arzt zu gehen. ...
j) That's a good idea. I'll/we'll do that. Thank you very much/thanks a lot.
k) Gute Besserung und auf Wiedersehen. /
Sie wünscht gute Besserung und sagt auf Wiedersehen.

Aufgabe 8

Hinweis: Übertrage wieder vom Englischen ins Deutsche und umgekehrt. Auch hier wird zusätzlich noch die Lösung mit Perspektivwechsel angegeben.

a) Guten Tag. Was kann ich für Sie tun? / Wie kann ich Ihnen helfen? /
Der Rezeptionist fragt, was er für Sie tun / wie er Ihnen helfen kann.
b) Good afternoon/Hello. My name is Schmidt/I'm Mr. Schmidt. I've made a reservation. /
Good afternoon. This is Mr. Schmidt./He's Mr. Schmidt. He's made a reservation.
c) Herr Schmidt, Ihre Reservierung ist vom 15. bis zum 18. August. Könnte ich bitte Ihren Pass/Ausweis und Ihre Kreditkarte haben? /
Sie haben vom 15. bis zum 18. August reserviert. Der Rezeptionist braucht Ihren Pass und Ihre Kreditkarte.
d) Here you are. Could you please wake me up tomorrow at 6 a.m./6 o'clock in the morning? /
Here you are. Could you please wake him up at ...?

e) Natürlich/Gerne. Hier ist Ihr Schlüssel. Ihr Zimmer hat die Nummer 223. Von 6 Uhr bis 10 Uhr gibt es Frühstück. Der Frühstücksraum befindet sich im Erdgeschoss.
f) Do I have a nice view of the city from my room, or can I see the Statue of Liberty? /
Does he have a nice view of the city from his room, or can he see the Statue of Liberty?
g) Es tut mir leid, aber Ihr Zimmer ist im zweiten Stock. Deshalb haben Sie dort nicht wirklich viel Aussicht. Aber ich denke, dass Sie das Zimmer trotzdem mögen werden, weil es ziemlich ruhig (gelegen) ist. Wissen Sie, ruhige Zimmer sind für New York nicht typisch. /
Es tut ihm leid, aber ... Deshalb haben Sie dort nicht wirklich viel Aussicht. Aber er denkt, dass Sie das Zimmer trotzdem mögen werden ... Ruhige Zimmer sind für New York nicht üblich/typisch.
h) No problem. Can I buy tickets for the musical "Lion King" at the hotel? /
Can Mr. Schmidt buy tickets for the musical "Lion King" at the hotel?
i) Es tut mir leid/Leider nein. Wir verkaufen keine Theaterkarten. Sie können diese in den Theatern am Broadway oder am Ticketstand am Times Square kaufen. /
Es tut ihm leid, aber hier im Hotel werden keine Theaterkarten verkauft. Sie können sie aber in ... kaufen.
j) Thank you. Goodbye.

Aufgabe 9

Hinweis: Dolmetsche zwischen der deutschen Touristin und der Verkäuferin. Auch hier wird zusätzlich noch die Lösung mit Perspektivwechsel angegeben.

a) Hallo, (wie) kann ich Ihnen helfen?
Die Verkäuferin fragt, ob sie Ihnen helfen kann.
b) Yes, I'd like to have the blue T-shirt in size L/Large, please./Could you give me this blue T-shirt in large, please?
Yes, she would like to have this blue T-shirt ...
c) Hier, bitte schön.
d) Where can I try it on? / Where can she try it on?
e) Die Umkleidekabinen sind dort drüben.
f) This T-shirt is too large (for me). Could I have a smaller one, please? /
This T-shirt is too large (for her). Could she have a smaller one, please?

g) This one fits. How much is it?

h) (Es kostet) 20 Pfund. Brauchen Sie sonst noch etwas?/Kann ich sonst noch etwas für Sie tun? /
(Es kostet) 20 Pfund. ... / Kann sie sonst noch etwas für Sie tun?

i) I'd like these postcards, please. Do you also sell stamps? /
She would like to have these postcards, too. Do you sell stamps?

j) Leider nein./Es tut mir leid. Die müssen Sie im Postamt kaufen. /
Leider nein. Die müssen Sie im Postamt kaufen.

k) What a pity. Anyway, thank you. Goodbye.

Aufgabe 10

Hinweis: Verbinde die Stichpunkte zu einem kurzen Vortrag. Achte darauf, dass du alle vorgegebenen Stichpunkte verwendest, und dass dein Vortrag einen roten Faden hat.

Telling about a trip

Last August my friend and his parents went on a holiday to England, where they went on a bike tour. They stayed in England for two weeks. They rented the bikes in Bristol. There they started the tour along the coast. They wanted to go camping as well, but they weren't able to because it was too cold. So they stayed in hotels instead. The weather was bad: They had only two sunny days and a lot of rain instead. In the end, my friend's bike was stolen at the train station. My friend was happy when the holiday was over.

Aufgabe 11

Hinweis: Bilde anhand der Stichpunkte Fragen und Antworten für das Verkaufsgespräch. Achte auch hier wieder darauf, dass dein Gespräch logisch aufgebaut ist.

Teacher: Hello, how can I help you?
You: Are there still tickets for "Star Wars" available?
Teacher: Yes, there are. How many would you like to have?
You: Three, please.
Teacher: The tickets for the back rows are £ 6 each, the tickets for the front rows £ 4. Which tickets would you like to have?
You: We would like to have the front row tickets for £ 4, please.
Teacher: Here you are. That's £ 12. Is there anything else I can do for you?
You: Yes, please. At what time does the film start?

Teacher: The film starts at 7 o'clock. That's in 20 minutes.
You: Where can we buy some popcorn and a coke?
Teacher: You can buy them at the bar over there. If you want to buy a film poster, you can get it here at the ticket counter. Do you want one?
You: No thanks, bye.

Aufgabe 12

✎ **Hinweis:** *Verbinde die Stichpunkte zu einem kurzen Dialog. Achte darauf, dass du alle vorgegebenen Stichpunkte verwendest und dass dein Dialog sinnvoll ist.*

You: Hi, where are you from?
Boy: Hi there, nice to meet you, our group is from Manchester, England.
You: Are you here on a holiday?
Boy: No, we're not. We are here for a student exchange with a German school.
You: Do you like the music?
Boy: Yeah, it's great!
You: You know what? I was about to go for a drink, do you want something?
Boy: Yes, I'd like a coke, please.
You: Sure, I'll get it.
Boy: By the way, what's your name? I'm Dylan.
You: I'm ... Just a moment, I'll be right back.

Qualifizierender Hauptschulabschluss Bayern 2012
Lösungen – Englisch

A Listening

- Allgemeiner Hinweis: *Die Hörtexte werden in der Prüfung auf CD dargeboten.*
- *Die Aufnahmen werden insgesamt zweimal ohne zusätzliche Erklärungen oder Un-*
- *terbrechungen abgespielt. Lies dir die Aufgaben vor dem Hören genau durch. Wäh-*
- *rend des Hörens, bzw. im Anschluss daran, bearbeitest du die zugehörigen Aufga-*
- *ben. Bei den Aufgaben (Tasks) 1 und 3 darfst du jeweils nur ein Kästchen pro Reihe*
- *ankreuzen. Markierst du mehrere Kästchen, bekommst du keinen Punkt für die je-*
- *weilige Teilaufgabe.*

Part 1

1 RECEPTIONIST: Hi, can I help you?
   PAUL: Hi, yeah, we wanted to know if we can book a boat trip.
   ALISON: And maybe you could recommend one to us.
   RECEPTIONIST: Sure. A lot of our guests do this one. *(Gets a brochure and opens it.)*
5 ALISON: Oh, dolphins!
   RECEPTIONIST: Yeah. This is a four-hour trip to watch the wild dolphins and their babies.
   PAUL: Great, and can we go in the water, too?
   RECEPTIONIST: Yeah, you can go snorkeling but not where the dolphins are, of
10   course.
   PAUL: Yeah, OK. And are there trips every day?
   RECEPTIONIST: Yeah, every day, leaving at 9 o'clock and getting back at around 1.30.
   ALISON: OK. And how much does it cost?
15 RECEPTIONIST: Well, it's usually $ 95 over the phone and 90 over the internet, but we can do it for you for 85.
   PAUL: OK.
   ALISON: And do we have to book in advance?
   RECEPTIONIST: You do, I'm afraid. The day before. Tomorrow's trip is almost full
20   but there's still space on Friday.
   PAUL: OK, we'll think about it and let you know.
   RECEPTIONIST: OK.
   PAUL AND ALISON: Thanks.

Vokabelhinweise: *Z. 3: to recommend: empfehlen; Z. 9: to snorkel: schnorcheln;*
Z. 18: in advance: im Voraus

1. watch dolphins.
   Hinweis: *Z. 6 f.*
2. snorkeling.
   Hinweis: *Z. 9*
3. 9 to 1.30.
   Hinweis: *Z. 12 f.*
4. $ 85.
   Hinweis: *Z. 16*
5. on Friday.
   Hinweis: *Z. 20*

Part 2

TV MAN: OK, and let's have a look at the weather coming up over the next three days. Today it's going to be partly cloudy with temperatures steady at around 75 Fahrenheit. The chance of rain is about 20 % and the easterly winds are going to be between 15 to 20 mph.
  Tomorrow, Thursday, it's going to feel quite breezy, too, with easterly winds between 25 to 30 mph. There's going to be a mix of sunshine and clouds. The chance of rain will be around 30 %, but all in all it'll feel warm out there with temperatures reaching a high of 85.
  Moving on to Friday now. Friday's going to start clear and bright but with easterly winds reaching 35 mph there's a 50 % chance of rain by the late afternoon. Temperatures are going to climb to a maximum of 95 and it's going to feel pretty humid, too.
  OK, so after the break, we'll be welcoming a special guest because *(fade begins here)* City Manager Billy Wardlow will be here to talk about the new parking regulations that are being introduced next year and what they're going to mean.

Vokabelhinweise:
Z. 2: *partly cloudy:* teilweise bewölkt; *steady:* gleichbleibend (konstant)
Z. 5: *breezy:* windig

	Temperature in Fahrenheit (°F)	Chance of rain in percent (%)	Winds in miles per hour (mph)
Today	75	20	15–20
Thursday	85	30	25–30
Friday	95	50	35

✏ **Hinweis:** *In den USA wird v. a. die Fahrenheit-Skala verwendet, um Temperaturen anzugeben: 75° Fahrenheit (Z. 3) = 23,9 °C, 85° Fahrenheit (Z. 8) = 29,4 °C, 95° Fahrenheit (Z. 11) = 35 °C.*
✏ In einigen englischsprachigen Ländern wird die Einheit mph (miles per hour) verwendet, um Geschwindigkeiten anzugeben: 35 mph (Z. 10) entsprechen rund 56 km/h.
✏ Die richtigen Lösungen findest du in folgenden Abschnitten: Today (Z. 2–4), Thursday (Z. 5–8), Friday (Z. 9–12)

Part 3

1 RECEPTIONIST: Hello there.
PAUL/ALISON: Hi.
RECEPTIONIST: Made up your mind about the boat trip yet?
PAUL: Yeah, we'd like to book for tomorrow if that's possible.
5 RECEPTIONIST: Oh, I'm sorry but tomorrow's trip's been cancelled because of the bad weather. How about Saturday?
ALISON: We're leaving on Saturday. Tomorrow's our last day.
RECEPTIONIST: Have you thought about going to *SeaWorld*?
PAUL: But that's quite a long way, isn't it?
10 RECEPTIONIST: Yeah, you're right, about 140 miles, so about 2 hours by car.
ALISON: Do you really want to be sitting in a car for four hours if we've got a 10-hour flight the next day?
PAUL: No, you're right.
ALISON: I'd rather be here tomorrow.
15 PAUL: And today? What else could we do?
RECEPTIONIST: Have you ever tried parasailing – you know, in a parachute from behind a boat?
ALISON: That sounds cool!
RECEPTIONIST: You can do it together – tandem parasailing.
20 PAUL: Locally?
RECEPTIONIST: Yes, there's a place about ten minutes on foot from here. I'll show you on the map where it is.
ALISON: Great. Then we can walk down there and check it out.
PAUL: That's a good idea.

Vokabelhinweise:
Z. 10: 140 miles: ca. 225 km
Z. 16: parachute: Fallschirm
Z. 20: locally: in der Nähe

1. False
   Hinweis: Z. 5 (*"tomorrow's trip's been cancelled"*)
2. True
   Hinweis: Z. 7
3. False
   Hinweis: Z. 10
4. True
   Hinweis: Z. 19
5. False
   Hinweis: Z. 21 (*"on foot"*)

Part 4

1 SUNRISE: Hi, how can I help?
ALISON: Hi, I wanted to ask if we can join one of your trips today.
SUNRISE: Sure. When do you want to go?
ALISON: Well, this afternoon would be great.
5 SUNRISE: How about 2 o'clock. Or 3 o'clock?
ALISON: Two's fine. Do we need to bring anything special with us?
SUNRISE: Well the usual stuff – a towel, sunscreen and sunglasses. Oh, and your camera, of course.
ALISON: And do you need to see our passports?
10 SUNRISE: No, no.
ALISON: No identification or anything?
SUNRISE: No, just the name of the hotel where you're staying.
ALISON: OK. Um ... oh yes: my boyfriend's a bit scared of heights so I wanted to know how high up we go.
15 SUNRISE: About 500 feet – but that's the maximum.
ALISON: Okay. And how long is the trip?
SUNRISE: About 45 minutes, and you're up in the air for about 10 minutes. But your boyfriend needn't worry. You'll be up there with him holding his hand!
Alison: True. I'll tell him that.

Vokabelhinweise:
Z. 7: *sunscreen: Sonnencreme*
Z. 11: *identification: Ausweis*
Z. 15: *500 feet: ca. 153 m*

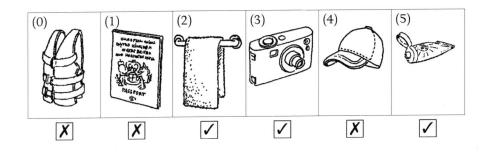

B Use of English

🖉 **Hinweis:** *In diesem Teil werden dein Wortschatz und deine Grammatik-Kenntnisse geprüft. Sind bei einer Aufgabe Wörter bereits vorgegeben, achte beim Einsetzen des ausgewählten Wortes in die Lücke darauf, das Wort richtig zu schreiben. Abschreibfehler führen nämlich zu Punktverlust, den du mit etwas Sorgfalt vermeiden kannst.*

Aufgabe 1

🖉 **Hinweis:** *Setze hier die passenden Wörter ein. Überlege dir, wie die einzelnen Wörter auf Deutsch heißen, denn einige dieser Namenwörter kann man auf Englisch leicht verwechseln, z. B. cloths (Tücher/Lappen) – clothes (Kleidung), counties (Grafschaften/Bezirke) – countries (Länder). Die schräg gedruckten Wörter im Text geben dir den Hinweis auf das fehlende Wort.*

Last year I travelled around the world for three <u>months</u> in *June, July and August*. I went to *Japan, India, the USA* and a lot of other <u>countries</u>. Of all the cities I saw I like New York best. When I was there I visited *the Empire State Building, the Statue of Liberty, Times Square* and many other well-known <u>sights</u>. I went to a fashion store and bought a *jacket, trousers, a shirt* and other <u>clothes</u> which are cheaper than in England. New York was full of tourists. I heard them speak *French, Chinese, Russian* and many other <u>languages</u>.

Aufgabe 2

🖉 **Hinweis:** *Hier musst du Wörter finden, die dieselbe Bedeutung haben wie die Wörter in Klammern.*

Woman: When does the show <u>finish</u> this evening?
Man: At about 10 o'clock.
Woman <u>Maybe</u> we can have dinner somewhere afterwards.

Man: Good idea.
Woman: Are there any restaurants close to the theatre?
Man: I don't think so. But we can <u>walk</u> somewhere.
Woman: No, let's <u>take</u> / <u>call</u> a taxi.
Man: OK.
Woman: And let's <u>book</u> a table.

Aufgabe 3

Hinweis: *Hier geht es darum, die richtige Form des angegebenen Verbs einzusetzen. Achte hier u. a. auf die grammatikalischen Zeiten (tenses) und die Signalwörter, nach denen eine bestimmte Form verwendet werden muss.*

Signalwort	Form	Zeit	Besonderheit
at the age of ten	learned	simple past	–
when	was	simple past	–
good at	swimming	–	-ing-Form nach „to be good <u>at</u>"
usually	wins	simple present	Mike win<u>s</u>
next year	will have, 'll have	will future	

At the age of ten I <u>learned</u> how to surf. When I got my own board I <u>was</u> so happy. Now I'm not only good at <u>surfing</u>. I'm also a very good swimmer. Every weekend my friend Mike and I meet at a lake. Often we race against each other and Mike usually <u>wins</u>. At the moment I'm saving for a special course in Spain. I hope that I <u>'ll have</u> / <u>will have</u> enough money next year.

Aufgabe 4

Hinweis: *Ergänze hier die Sätze mit den richtigen Wörtern aus dem Kasten. Achte dabei auf den Textzusammenhang.*

Jack and his sister Tina spent a weekend <u>in</u> London. When they got <u>to</u> the station, Jack carried his sister's suitcase <u>because</u> it was so heavy. They took the Underground to <u>their</u> aunt. She lives in a small flat all by herself and she is a great cook. Whenever she <u>has</u> guests, she likes to cook for them.

Aufgabe 5

Hinweis: *Hier musst du einen Dialog ergänzen. Mithilfe der vorgegebenen Antworten kannst du die fehlenden Fragen erschließen.*

Tina:	Excuse me? <u>Can you help me</u>?
Londoner:	Yes, of course.
Tina:	<u>Is there a bus</u> / <u>Is this the bus</u> / <u>Could you tell me if there is a bus</u> / <u>Do you know if there is a bus</u> to the Tower?
Londoner:	Yes, it's bus number 15.
Tina:	How long <u>does it take</u> / <u>will it take</u> / <u>will it be</u> to get there?
Londoner:	Not long. About twenty minutes.
Tina:	How <u>much is it</u> / <u>much does it cost</u> / <u>much is the ticket</u>?
Londoner:	I'm not sure but the driver will know the price.
Tina:	<u>Do you know</u> / <u>Would you tell me</u> / <u>Could you tell me</u> if there's a bus stop nearby?
Londoner:	Yes, just around the corner.
Tina:	Thank you.
Londoner:	No worries.

C Reading Comprehension

Allgemeiner Hinweis: *Lies den Text erst einmal durch, damit du weißt, wovon er handelt. Sieh dir die Aufgaben an und suche die Stellen im Text, die dir den Hinweis auf die richtige Lösung geben.*

Vokabelhinweise:

Z. 8: *to take part in:* teilnehmen an
Z. 8 f.: *state-wide surf competition:* Surf-Wettbewerb mit Teilnehmern aus den einzelnen Bundesstaaten der USA
Z. 10: *passion:* Leidenschaft
Z. 13: *15-foot tiger shark:* 4,5 m langer Tigerhai
Z. 16: *to recover:* sich erholen
Z. 17: *physically:* körperlich
Z. 17: *mentally:* seelisch
Z. 17: *attitude:* Einstellung
Z. 18: *faith:* Glaube
Z. 26: *success:* Erfolg
Z. 34: *foundation:* Stiftung
Z. 35: *non-profit:* gemeinnützig, nicht auf Gewinn ausgerichtet
Z. 35: *to support:* unterstützen
Z. 35: *survivor:* Überlebende(r)

Aufgabe 1

Hinweis: Finde hier zu jedem Absatz die passende Überschrift.

paragraph 1 (lines 1–10)	paragraph 2 (lines 11–15)	paragraph 3 (lines 16–20)	paragraph 4 (lines 21–28)	paragraph 5 (lines 29–36)	paragraph 6 (lines 37–40)
E	C	D	G	A	B

Aufgabe 2

Hinweis: Im Lesetext über Bethany Hamilton fehlen vier Sätze. Diese sind im Text mit (1), (2), (3) und (4) gekennzeichnet. Die fehlenden Sätze (sowie einen weiteren, nicht passenden Satz) findest du in Aufgabe 2. Erschließe aus dem Zusammenhang, welcher Satz zu welcher Textstelle passt und trage den jeweiligen Buchstaben in die Tabelle ein.

Hinweise im Text:

(1) F: "I was more scared..." (Z. 19 f.)
(2) A: "... surfing competitions have taken her to South America, ..." (Z. 25 f.)
(3) C: "Bethany is not only a star in the water." (Z. 29)
(4) D: "This is what she has to say to young people: ..." (Z. 39)

Vokabelhinweise:

to compete with: sich messen mit, gegen jmd. antreten
successful: erfolgreich
to be hopeless: ohne Hoffnung sein

(0)	(1)	(2)	(3)	(4)
B	F	A	C	D

Aufgabe 3

Hinweis: Überprüfe hier, ob die Aussagen zum Lesetext richtig oder falsch sind.

a) True
   Hinweis: Z. 4 f.

b) False
   Hinweis: Z. 13 f.

c) False
Hinweis: Z. 18 f.
d) True
Hinweis: Z. 39 f.

Aufgabe 4

a)	b)	c)	d)
line(s) 6–7	line(s) 11–12	line(s) 17–18	line(s) 29–30

Aufgabe 5

a) (in) 2005
Hinweis: Z. 22 f.
b) (it's) Soul Surfer
Hinweis: Z. 31
c) shark attack survivors
oder: (other) amputees (worldwide)
Hinweis: Z. 35 f.

D Text Production

Allgemeiner Hinweis: *Auch in diesem Prüfungsteil darfst du ein zweisprachiges Wörterbuch verwenden. Entscheide dich bei der Bearbeitung entweder für die E-Mail oder für die Bildergeschichte.*

1. Correspondence: E-Mail

Hinweis: *Berücksichtige beim Verfassen deiner E-Mail die allgemeinen Hinweise zu Umfang und Form, die in der Aufgabenstellung beschrieben sind. Verfasse eine verständliche E-Mail in ganzen Sätzen. Bringe beim Schreiben die Vorgaben zum Inhalt ein und ergänze sie, wenn du möchtest, auch durch eigene Gedanken.*

Hi Chris,

Would you like to take part in an international football (*oder AmE:* soccer) camp with me? I went to an international football camp in London last summer and it was great! I stayed there for two weeks and I was able to improve my skills a lot. It was the first time that I got training from professional trainers and I also met some football stars! Just imagine, I even shook hands with Theo Walcott and I also got some autographs!

It was also great that I was able to meet other boys and girls from all over the world. At the weekends we went sightseeing in London. We visited the Emirates stadium, went shopping and one night we went to a fantastic disco.

I am going to apply *(bewerben)* for the football camp again this year. Do you want to join me? You can find some more information on the internet: www.soccer-campsinternational.com/arsenal-soccer-camp

I'm looking forward to hearing from you soon.

Best wishes,
Angela

2. Picture-based Writing:

Hinweis: *Sieh dir die Bilder genau an, bevor du mit dem Schreiben beginnst. Beachte auch die Aufschriften: „Happy birthday", „remote controlled shark" (ferngesteuerter Hai), „lifeguard" (Rettungsschwimmer), „Help!" und „Ron's pedal boat". Berücksichtige beim Schreiben der Bildergeschichte die allgemeinen Hinweise zu Umfang und Form, die in der Aufgabenstellung angegeben sind. Denke an Einleitung, Überleitung und Schluss und verwende in deinem Text auch die wörtliche Rede. Wie die Geschichte beginnen könnte, findest du ebenfalls auf dem Angabenblatt. Verfasse die Geschichte in der Zeitform <u>simple past</u> (Signalwort: last year).*

Shark alarm

Paul always wanted to have a remote-controlled shark. Last year, on his birthday, he finally got one as a present from his parents. He was very happy. Paul took the shark with him the next time he went to the seaside. It was a sunny and warm day and some people were out on the sea in pedal boats. "The perfect moment to try my remote-controlled shark", Paul thought. He wanted to scare the people a little by letting the shark swim around their pedal boats. It worked wonderfully! Two ladies with hats got really frightened when they saw the shark's fin *(Flosse)* going around their boat. One of them threw her arms up into the air and the other one screamed "Help!" The life guard came right away and was very angry with Paul. "Leave the beach – now! You are not allowed to come back with your shark anymore!" he shouted. Paul was disappointed that the life guard didn't see the fun of it.

Notenschlüssel

Notenstufen	1	2	3	4	5	6
Punkte	80–68	67–55	54–41	40–27	26–13	12–0

Qualifizierender Abschluss der Mittelschule Bayern 2013
Lösungen – Englisch

A Listening

Allgemeiner Hinweis: *Die Hörtexte werden in der Prüfung von einer CD abgespielt, und zwar insgesamt zweimal und ohne zusätzliche Erklärungen oder Unterbrechungen. Du bekommst Zeit, dir die Aufgaben anzusehen, bevor du den dazugehörigen Text das erste Mal hörst. Während des Zuhörens, bzw. im Anschluss daran, bearbeitest du dann die jeweilige Aufgabe.*

Part 1

1 WAITER: Yours was the white wine, wasn't it, madam?
MOTHER: Um, no, that was for my husband. The red is for me.
WAITER: I'm sorry, here you are madam.
MOTHER: Thanks.
5 WAITER: And the white for you, sir.
FATHER: Thank you.
WAITER: Roast beef with chips and mixed vegetables. Is this for you, sir?
FATHER: Er, no. It's for my daughter. I ordered the fish.
WAITER: Ah, the fish. The fish with rice and broccoli.
10 FATHER: Right.
WAITER: Here you are, young lady. Your roast beef. Enjoy your meal.
RACHEL: Thank you.
MOTHER: Hmm ... that looks fantastic. I should have taken that, too, but I'm sure my fish soup will be fine.
15 WAITER: Okay, fish with rice and broccoli. Here you are, sir. And the soup for you, madam. Hope you enjoy it.
FATHER & MOTHER: Thank you.

	mother	father	daughter
white wine		✓	
red wine	✓		
fish		✓	
fish soup	✓		
rice		✓	

	mother	father	daughter
broccoli		✓	
beef steak			
roast beef			✓
chips			✓
vegetables			✓
vegetable soup			
	1 point	1 point	1 point

/ **Hinweis:** *In der Auswahlliste findest du zwei Gerichte („beef steak" und „vegetable
/ soup"), die im Hörtext nicht vorkommen.*

Part 2

1 SPEAKER: ... and in our restaurant we have a wide selection of meals today.
Come to our Sandwich Corner and create your own sandwich! Choose from a variety of bread and a range of meats and cheeses. Every sandwich costs just £ 2.50.
5 Today's special offer in the Sandwich Corner and only available between four and five this afternoon: buy one and get one free!
At our Salad Bar, you can make your own salad for only £ 3.99. Pay just £ 1 more, and you can choose from a selection of cold ham, sausages, eggs and fish to go with your salad.
10 If you prefer a warm meal, Italian food is our speciality this week. We offer some of the most popular Italian dishes. Prices start at £ 4.50. For children we have halfprice meals for only £ 2.25.
These delicious offers are all available now in our restaurant. Come and join us on the fifth floor.

Vokabelhinweise:
Z. 1: *selection: Auswahl*
Z. 5: *available: erhältlich*
Z. 10: *to prefer: etw. vorziehen*
Z. 14: *floor: Etage, Stockwerk*

1. From **4** to **5** o'clock you get two sandwiches and pay for only one.
2. Creating your own salad costs £ **3.99**.
3. Pay only £ **1** more and you can add ham or eggs to your salad.
4. The cheapest warm meal is £ **4.50**.
5. Children can have an Italian dish for £ **2.25**.
6. The restaurant is on the **5(th)** floor.

Part 3

ANNE: Mmm, this soup tastes delicious. Did you make it yourself?
BETTY: Yes, but it's nothing special, just my usual cream of vegetable soup.
ANNE: But it really is fantastic. What did you put in it?
BETTY: Well, some chopped cabbage, a bit of celery, carrots, and some fried onions.
5   And then I added spices, of course, and salt and pepper and so on …
ANNE: Hmm, but this has got potatoes and tomatoes in it, hasn't it?
BETTY: Yes, potatoes, I always use them. And I normally use tomatoes too, but I didn't have any today.
ANNE: And the green bits? What are they? Beans?
10 BETTY: No, no, they're peas.
ANNE: Hmm, and there's no meat in it?
BETTY: No, there is. I put a bit of bacon in it. Is that okay for you?
ANNE: Yeah, of course. It gives it a really lovely flavour.
BETTY: Yes. I think so, too.
15 ANNE: Are all the vegetables from your garden?
BETTY: Yes, everything. Only one thing isn't: the mushrooms.
ANNE: Well, it really is delicious.
BETTY: Thank you. Would you like some more?

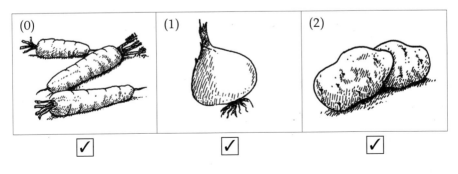

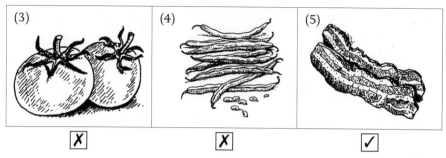

🖋 **Hinweis:** *Kreuze hier unbedingt <u>sowohl</u> die Zutaten an, die in der Gemüsesuppe enthalten (✓), <u>als auch</u> solche, die <u>nicht</u> (✗) enthalten sind. Es darf kein Kästchen leer bleiben!*

Part 4

1   PAMELA: Hello.
    MIKE: Hi, Pamela. It's me, Mike.
    PAMELA: Hi, Mike, nice to hear from you again. Are you back?
    MIKE: Yes, I've been back since Monday. I thought it would be nice to meet up for
5   a meal again. How about Friday evening?
    PAMELA: Well, that's a nice idea, Mike, but I'm afraid I'm rather busy right now.
        On Friday I probably won't be home until 9 or something…
    MIKE: Oh, I see. Well, what about Saturday, then?
    PAMELA: That sounds fine. Where would you like to go?
10 MIKE: Well, what do you think about an Indian restaurant? Shall we try one?
    PAMELA: I'm sorry, but Indian food is far too hot for me.
    MIKE: Okay. Why don't we go to the Red Lion, then? They do good food, and
        they have a lot of vegetarian meals. Have you been there? Do you know the pub?
    PAMELA: Yes, I know it well. Everybody goes there for their fresh vegetables and
15   baked potatoes. Let's go there. How about 7 o'clock?
    MIKE: I think it opens at 7, so I'll pick you up at your house at half past six. Okay?
    PAMELA: Fine. See you on Saturday then.
    MIKE: Thanks. Bye now.
    PAMELA: Bye, Mike.

		T	F
1.	He wants to go out on Friday.	✓	
2.	Pamela wants to stay at home till 9.		✓
3.	She likes hot Indian meals.		✓

	T	F
4. The Red Lion pub is popular because of its baked potatoes.	✓	
5. The pub is closed till 7.	✓	
6. Mike wants to pick Pamela up at 7.30.		✓

B Use of English

🖊 **Hinweis:** *In diesem Teil werden deine Grammatik- und Wortschatzkenntnisse sowie deine Kenntnisse der Redemittel geprüft. Beachte auch die Rechtschreibung, vor allem dann, wenn die Wörter wie in Aufgabe 3 schon vorgegeben sind.*

Aufgabe 1

🖊 **Hinweis:** *Die Abfolge der Bilder und Sätze stimmt nicht überein. Lies zunächst die Sätze durch, suche dann das Bild, das vom Sinn her passen könnte und schreibe schließlich das entsprechende Wort dafür in die Lücke. Bild 4 („chicken" oder „turkey") wird nicht gebraucht.*

Tom is having a <u>party</u>. A lot of <u>guests</u>/<u>people</u>/<u>friends</u> are coming. Everything is ready. The <u>plates</u> are on the table. The <u>fridge</u>/<u>refrigerator</u>/<u>freezer</u> is full of food and there is enough pizza for everybody. But one thing is missing – the <u>chocolate</u> cake Tom's sister wanted to make for him.

Aufgabe 2

🖊 **Hinweis:** *Bei dieser Übung ist es hilfreich, nach <u>Signalwörtern</u> zu suchen, die dir einen Hinweis auf die richtige Zeitform geben:*
Signalwörter: Zeitform:
fifty years ago   →   simple past
since   →   present perfect
today   →   simple present
Falls du dir bei dieser Aufgabe unsicher warst, kannst du in der Kurzgrammatik im Band „Training Quali" auf S. 90 ff. nachschlagen. Verwende im 2. Satz nach „if" („wenn/falls") auch das „simple past", da sich alles in der Vergangenheit abspielt.

Food from other countries <u>has become</u> very popular in Britain. Fifty years ago most people <u>went</u> to a pub if they <u>didn't want</u> to eat at home. Since the 1980s a lot of foreign restaurants <u>have opened</u> all over Britain. Today, there <u>are</u> Chinese restaurants everywhere.

Aufgabe 3

Hinweis: *Hier musst du die Wörter in die richtige Reihenfolge bringen und jeweils einen sinnvollen Satz bilden. Manchmal gibt es verschiedene Möglichkeiten.*

1. Have you ever been to the restaurant near the station?
2. Yes, I have already been there three times this month. / Yes, I have been there three times this month already. / Yes, I have been there already three times this month.
3. What is the food there like? / What is the food like there?
4. The food is great/cheap but not cheap/great. / The food is not great/cheap but cheap/great.

Aufgabe 4

Hinweis: *Kreise das Wort ein, das grammatikalisch oder sinngemäß passt. Nur ein Wort pro Auswahlreihe ist richtig.*
Vokabelhinweise zu den richtigen Lösungen:
usually: normalerweise, gewöhnlich
there: dort
which: leitet hier einen Relativsatz ein (... eine Mahlzeit, <u>die</u> ...); „who" wird nur bei Personen verwendet; „what" ist ein Fragewort (was?); „whose" bezeichnet den Genitiv (dessen/wessen)
with other pupils: mit anderen Schülern
to enjoy themselves: sich amüsieren, hier im Sinn von: „eine gute Zeit haben"

British pupils (0) • almost • nearly • suddenly • ☐usually☐ • have lunch in their school cafeteria. (1) • That • Their • ☐There☐ • Where • they can get drinks, snacks or even a meal (2) • what • ☐which☐ • who • whose • is quite cheap. They sit together with (3) • a • another • ☐other☐ • our • pupils from their class, have a chat and enjoy (4) • each other • them • ☐themselves☐ • they • before they go to their afternoon lessons.

Aufgabe 5

Hinweis: *Lies dir zunächst Toms Antworten durch. Notiere dann eine passende Frage. Meist gibt es mehrere richtige Möglichkeiten.*

Peter: Hi, Tom. How are you?
Tom: I'm fine. I'm on a trip through Germany.
Peter: Oh. Where are you?
Tom In Munich. I'm staying in a hostel.
Peter: OK. How much does it cost? / How much is it per night? / …?
Tom: € 28 per night, which is not bad.
Peter: Great. What's the weather like? / How is the weather? / What about the weather? / …
Tom: It's sunny and warm.
Peter: Lovely. When will you be back (home)? / When are you coming back / home? / …?
Tom: I'll be back next weekend.
Peter: Great. See you then. Have fun.
Tom: Thanks. Bye.

C Reading Comprehension

Allgemeiner Hinweis: *Lies den Text zunächst einmal durch, damit du weißt, wovon er handelt. Schlage nur diejenigen unbekannten Wörter nach, die zum Verständnis des Textes unbedingt nötig sind. Nimm dir Zeit beim Durchsehen der Aufgaben, damit du verstehst, welche Lösung gesucht ist. Hier lohnt es sich, das ein oder andere Wort nachzuschlagen. Konzentriere dich nun auf die Stellen im Text, die zur Beantwortung der jeweiligen Aufgabe von Bedeutung sind.*

Vokabelhinweise:

Z. 2 f.: inhabitant: Einwohner
Z. 3: port: Hafen
Z. 5: to invent: erfinden
Z. 6: Earl: Graf
Z. 7: to command the Navy: die Kriegsflotte/Marine kommandieren
Z. 11: slice: Scheibe
Z. 13: convenient: praktisch, bequem
Z. 18: cucumber: Gurke
Z. 24: competition: Wettbewerb
Z. 26: groceries: Lebensmittel
Z. 31: weight: Gewicht

Aufgabe 1

Hinweis: *Notiere die passende Überschrift zum jeweiligen Abschnitt des Lesetextes. Schreibe auch auf, welche Überschrift übrig bleibt („extra title").*

paragraph 1 (lines 1–4)	paragraph 2 (lines 5–14)	paragraph 3 (lines 15–20)	paragraph 4 (lines 21–29)	paragraph 5 (lines 30–36)	The extra title is
D	F	A	E	B	C

Aufgabe 2

Hinweis: *Kreuze an, ob die Aussage richtig (true: T), falsch (false: F) oder nicht im Text (not in the text: N) ist.*

                                               T F N

1. The distance between Sandwich and London is 18 miles. ☐ ✓ ☐
   Hinweis: Z. 1 f.
2. John Montagu often won when he played cards. ☐ ☐ ✓
3. Working men prefer cucumber sandwiches. ☐ ✓ ☐
   Hinweis: Z. 18 f.
4. Max King took part in a sandwich-making competition. ☐ ☐ ✓
5. A study shows that eating fast food can make you overweight. ✓ ☐ ☐
   Hinweis: Z. 30 f.
6. Mr Brightman, the owner of a sandwich restaurant, is married. ✓ ☐ ☐
   Hinweis: Z. 32 f.

Aufgabe 3

Hinweis: *Antworte in kurzen Sätzen oder Stichpunkten. Schreibe keine vollständigen Sätze aus dem Text ab.*

1. 5,000 / 5000
   Hinweis: Z. 2
2. he commanded the British Navy
   Hinweis: Z. 7
3. playing cards / (he loved to) play cards
   Hinweis: Z. 8

4. (because) he wanted to hold his cards and eat at the same time / (because) he wanted to play (cards) and eat at the same time / (because) he wanted to eat without (a) knife and (a) fork
   Hinweis: Z. 9 ff.
5. (because) they saw how convenient it was / (they saw) it was convenient
   Hinweis: Z. 12 f.
6. (a) butty
   Hinweis: Z. 19
7. (because) the smell gets into the bread/into it
   Hinweis: Z. 26 f.
8. freshly-baked bread / (filling of) organic vegetables / meat straight out of the oven
   Hinweis: Z. 34 ff. (delicious: lecker, köstlich)

D Text Production

Allgemeiner Hinweis: *Schreibe <u>entweder</u> die E-Mail <u>oder</u> die Bildergeschichte. Du darfst ein zweisprachiges Wörterbuch verwenden. Die Lösungsbeispiele sind bewusst etwas länger gehalten als in den Angaben vorgegeben. So bekommst du verschiedene Ideen für deine eigene Lösung.*

1. Correspondence: E-Mail

Hinweis: *Berücksichtige beim Schreiben deiner E-Mail die Vorgaben zu Umfang, Form und Inhalt, wie sie in der Aufgabenstellung aufgeführt sind. Da du die E-Mail an deine Gasteltern sendest, sollte sie <u>persönlichen</u> Charakter haben. Schreibe in ganzen Sätzen und achte darauf, dass deine E-Mail in sich schlüssig und verständlich ist. Der folgende Wortschatz kann dir beim Verfassen der E-Mail nützlich sein:*
- *Anrede: Dear ... / Hello, ...*
- *sich für die Zeit in der Gastfamilie bedanken: Thanks that I could ...*
- *Gefallen ausdrücken: It was great that ... / I liked ... / It was very nice that ...*
- *Unterkunft: accommodation, room, house, garden, balcony etc.*
- *Essen: breakfast, lunch, dinner*
- *Haustiere: pets (e.g. dog, cat, budgie, guinea pig), to pet, to feed, to go for a walk, well-bred (gut erzogen), cute (niedlich)*
- *Aktivitäten: sports (e.g. swimming, cycling, jogging, playing football), go to the cinema, play an instrument etc.*
- *Fotos im Anhang: to attach some photos*

- *von der Heimreise berichten:* to go by plane, to take ... hours, I arrived at ...
- *zuhause ankommen:* come back, return
- *Reaktionen schildern:* to be (not) pleased about, to be (not) happy about, to be (not) fond of, to like/dislike/love, to be (not) delighted
- *hoffen, dass die Gastfamilie zu Besuch kommt:* I hope/wish that you will come to see me; you're always welcome in my/our house
- *Grußformel:* Hope to hear from you soon, Regards, Best wishes, Lots of love, Bye, Take care, Yours ...

Dear Sarah and Paul,

How are you? I hope everybody is fine.

Thanks again that I could stay with you! You made me feel so comfortable. I liked my room very much. I also loved to sit on the balcony and look at all the pretty flowers in your garden. And of course I miss Kitty, your cute little cat that came over to visit me every morning. It was also so much fun to go to the pub, the cinema or the Art Festival in the evening. I have attached some photos – and I hope you like them, too.

My trip back home was okay. The plane was on time so that I arrived in the early afternoon. My family picked me up at the airport. My parents are happy that I'm back home again and my mother is very pleased about the earrings that I bought for her at the festival. But my brother doesn't like the T-Shirt I gave him as a present. He doesn't know much about fashion ... ☺!

I hope that you'll be able to see my family and me when you come to Germany next year. You're always welcome and I'm really looking forward to meeting you again.

Hope to hear from you soon.

Take care!

Yours, Isabel

2. Picture-based Writing:

Hinweis: *Berücksichtige beim Schreiben der Bildergeschichte die Vorgaben zu Umfang und Form, die in der Aufgabenstellung angegeben sind. Schreibe die Geschichte in der Zeitform „simple past" (One afternoon, Emily <u>called</u> Chris ...), zum Teil musst du die Verlaufsform („past progressive form") verwenden. Betrachte alle Bilder genau, damit du keine wichtigen Details übersiehst (z. B. in Bild 4: Uhr; unbemerktes Hereinschleichen der Katzen ins Esszimmer). Auch der Text und die Symbole in den Sprechblasen enthalten wichtige Informationen.*

Denke beim Schreiben an die Einleitung und den Schluss-Satz sowie an die Verwen-

dung der wörtlichen Rede. Schreibe in ganzen Sätzen, baue den Handlungsverlauf logisch auf und achte darauf, dass die Geschichte auch sprachlich gut verständlich ist.
- Der folgende Wortschatz kann dir beim Verfassen der Geschichte nützlich sein:
- Bild 1: verliebt sein in: be in love with, einladen: to invite, Einladung: invitation, die Katzen schliefen in ihren Körbchen: the cats <u>were sleeping</u> in their baskets
- Bild 2: kochen: to cook, Schüssel: bowl, Herd: stove, Ofen: oven, sich interessieren für: to be interested in, beobachten: to watch
- Bild 3: den Bus verpassen: to miss the bus, den Tisch decken: to lay the table/to set the table, anrufen: to call/to phone
- Bild 4: sich beeilen: to hurry, hereinschleichen: to sneak in, to crawl inside
- Bild 5: Unordnung: mess

Dinner for two

One afternoon, Emily called Chris to invite him for dinner. She asked him to come the following day at 8 pm. Chris was in love with Emily and was happy about the invitation. While Emily was talking to Chris, her two cats, Jerry and Johnny were sleeping in their baskets.

The next day, Emily was in her kitchen preparing the meal. She had a big fish in the oven, a pot with potatoes on the stove and a large bowl full of salad on the kitchen counter. Her two cats were watching her the whole time.

Just before 8 pm, Chris called Emily. He sounded disappointed. "I'm sorry, but I missed the bus!" he told her. Emily was already putting all the nice food on the table, but she said: "No worries, I'll pick you up, Chris." Emily left the dining room in a hurry, so she did not see that Johnny and Jerry had crawled inside before she closed the door. They were very hungry.

At 8 pm it was dinner time. Jerry and Johnny were sharing the fish on the table. They just loved it! For poor Emily and Chris they only left the potatoes and the salad, which were lying on the floor.

Notenschlüssel

Notenstufen	1	2	3	4	5	6
Punkte	80–71	70–60	59–46	45–32	31–18	17–0

> **Qualifizierender Abschluss der Mittelschule Bayern 2014**
> **Lösungen – Englisch**

A Listening

Allgemeiner Hinweis: *Der Hörverstehenstest besteht aus drei Teilen. In dem Test geht es um ein Paar, das in den USA Urlaub macht. Zu jedem Text, den du von der CD hörst, gibt es eine Aufgabe („Task"), die du mithilfe der Informationen aus dem jeweiligen Hörtext bearbeiten sollst.*
Verschaffe dir zuerst einen Überblick über die Aufgaben. Du hörst die Texte je zwei Mal. Du kannst die Aufgaben entweder während des Zuhörens und/oder im Anschluss daran bearbeiten.

Part 1

1 MIKE/KATE: Hello. Hi.
RECEPTIONIST: Hello there. Can I help you?
MIKE: Yes, we've reserved a room ... um ... on the internet.
RECEPTIONIST: OK. Could I have your passports, please?
5 KATE: Sure.
RECEPTIONIST: Is this your first stay here?
MIKE: Well, not in the US, but it's our first visit to Washington.
RECEPTIONIST: OK. Great. Three nights, right. Leaving on Friday.
KATE: Yeah. That's right.
10 RECEPTIONIST: Could I have your credit card, please?
MIKE: Sure.
KATE: Um ... we wanted to know if you had a room at the back, you know, away from the road.
RECEPTIONIST: Well, actually, you're in room 430, which *is* at the back.
15 MIKE: Great. Thanks. And all the rooms have Wi-Fi, don't they?
RECEPTIONIST: Yes, they do. You'll need the password, it's JFK 430.
KATE: Great. Thanks. Um ... we're booked on a tour of the White House tomorrow morning.
MIKE: Yeah, is it far from here?
20 RECEPTIONIST: Actually it is. But you can take a taxi or a bus. There's a bus stop right outside the hotel.
MIKE: OK. What about breakfast?
RECEPTIONIST: Breakfast is served from 6.30 till 10. The breakfast room's in the basement. The elevator is behind the bar, on your right.
25 KATE: OK, thanks.
RECEPTIONIST: Enjoy your stay.

1. The receptionist wants to see their **passport(s)/(credit card)**.
   Hinweis: Z. 4/Z. 10
2. It's Kate and Mike's **first/1st** visit to Washington DC.
   Hinweis: Z. 7
3. They are leaving on **Friday**.
   Hinweis: Z. 8
4. They would like a room which is at **the back** of the hotel.
   Hinweis: Z. 12
5. The Wi-Fi password is **JFK 430**.
   Hinweis: Z. 16; konzentriere dich hier besonders, um die Buchstaben-Zahlen-Kombination richtig zu verstehen.
6. They should take a **taxi** or a bus to get to the White House.
   Hinweis: Z. 20
7. The bus stop is **(right) outside** the hotel.
   Hinweis: Z. 20
8. Breakfast is from **6.30** till **10**.
   Hinweis: Z. 23

Part 2

1   GUIDE: Welcome to the White House. Our tour begins with some history. It took eight years to build the White House, from 1792 to 1800. Today the White House is where the president and his family live but it is also where he and his staff, over 1,500 people, work. It has 132 rooms on 6 floors. Here are some
5   more figures about the White House. *(Fade begins)* There are ...
   GUIDE: You're now standing in the Map Room. On the walls you can see different maps of Washington DC and the world. Today meetings, television interviews, small teas or even classical concerts are held here. *(Fade begins)* It was ...
10 GUIDE: If you look out of the window you'll see a tennis court. Soon after Barack Obama became president, it was changed so that people could play basketball on it as well. President Obama is a big basketball fan. He does not play alone, though. He often invites school teams, college teams and also professionals to play at the White House. *(Fade begins)* It is ...
15 GUIDE: Also outside you'll see one of the White House's latest projects: the First Lady's garden. Here Mrs Obama is growing vegetables so that her family – but also guests – get fresh vegetables. Mrs Obama hopes the garden will be a learn-

ing experience where visitors to the White House can see how fresh food can be part of a healthy diet. *(Fade begins)* If you ...

20 GUIDE: This is the White House Library. The room was not always full of books and paintings. Many years ago it was a laundry room, where the first families' clothes were washed, dried and ironed. *(Fade begins)* If you ...

GUIDE: You are now in the Family Theater. This is a movie theater with 42 seats where the First Family and their guests can watch movies, sports games and
25 TV shows. *(Fade begins)* In March ...

Allgemeiner Hinweis: *Folgende Fragewörter solltest du verstehen, um die Fragen richtig beantworten zu können:*
- how many? – wie viele?
- where? – wo?
- who? – wer?
- what? – was?

1. 132
   - Hinweis: Z. 4
2. (on the) wall(s)
   - Hinweis: Z. 6
3. school teams/college teams/professionals
   - Hinweis: Z. 13
4. (the) garden (project)
   - Hinweis: Z. 17 f.
5. paintings
   - Hinweis: Z. 21 (except = außer)
6. (in the) Family Theater/movie theater/Theater
   - Hinweis: Z. 23

Part 3

MIKE: You know my idea about hiking through the Grand Canyon in one day?
KATE: Yeah.
MIKE: Well, we can forget that. It takes 12 hours to go down one side and up the other. And it's really hot down there at this time of the year. Over 35° in some places.
KATE: Can't we camp for one night?
MIKE: Camp? No, we'd need a special permit to do that. And it's too late to get one now anyway.
KATE: Oh. OK.
MIKE: I've got another idea, though. We could go on a helicopter tour. There's one here. You fly through the Grand Canyon, land somewhere, have a picnic and then fly back. Three hours in total.
KATE: But what does it cost?
MIKE: Hold on. Oh. Mmm. Ah, 499 dollars per person.
KATE: Well, that's expensive for 3 hours.
MIKE: Here's another tour. Wait a second. OK, this one goes from Grand Canyon Airport and lasts about 30 minutes. But you don't land anywhere.
KATE: Is that cheaper?
MIKE: Hold on. It says ... 199 dollars ... no, wait ... 154 dollars if you book on-line.
KATE: Sounds cool, doesn't it?
MIKE: Shall I book?
KATE: Yeah.
MIKE: When are we at the Grand Canyon?
KATE: On Monday.
MIKE: OK. How about booking for Tuesday at ... er 10.30?
KATE: Sounds perfect.
MIKE: Great.

	Hiking tour	Helicopter tour	Tour from Grand Canyon Airport
Costs per person?	No costs	$ 499 (Z. 14)	$ 154 online booking (Z. 19 f.)
Hours/minutes?	12 hours (Z. 3)	3 hours	30 minutes (Z. 16 f.)
Problems?	(really) hot/35° (Z. 4 f.)/ (need a) permit (Z. 7) (for camping)	(too) expensive (Z. 15)	no stop in the Canyon

B Use of English

Allgemeiner Hinweis: *In diesem Prüfungsteil musst du dein Wissen im Bereich Wortschatz, Grammatik und Rechtschreibung unter Beweis stellen. Auch musst du eine Sprechsituation bewältigen, wie sie im Alltag vorkommen kann.*

Aufgabe 1

Hinweis: *In dieser Aufgabe werden deine Wortschatz- und Grammatikkenntnisse geprüft. Du findest bereits eine Auswahl an Wörtern im Kasten. Wähle die passenden aus. Im Folgenden findest du Hinweise zu den richtigen Lösungen:*
1. *who: leitet hier einen Relativsatz ein („... die bereits einen Studienplatz an einem College hat."); „which" ist hier nicht möglich, da es sich bei Julia um eine Person handelt. Siehe auch S. 87 f. in der Kurzgrammatik.*
2. *She ... enjoys working on the computer: sie arbeitet gerne am Computer (enjoy + Verb mit -ing-Form).*
3. *to be good at: gut sein in*
4. *got: simple past von „get" (bekommen)*
5. *would like: würde gerne*
6. *to apply for: sich bewerben für/um*

Julia, 17, is one (0) <u>of</u> the students at her high school (1) <u>who</u> has already got a place at college. She really enjoys (2) <u>working</u> on the computer and she's very good (3) <u>at</u> designing websites. On her last birthday she (4) <u>got</u> a new computer from her parents. In her vacation Julia (5) <u>would</u> like to do work experience at a software firm in Boston. She has already applied (6) <u>for</u> a job at three different companies but she's still waiting to hear from them.

Aufgabe 2

Hinweis: *Hier geht es nur um den Wortschatz. Ergänze den Lückentext mit den passenden Substantiven (Namenwörtern). Versuche, die fehlenden Wörter aus dem Textzusammenhang zu erschließen. Auch sind als Hilfestellung die Anfangsbuchstaben der gesuchten Wörter angegeben*
1. *satchel: Schultasche; schedule: hier: Stundenplan*
2. *dictionary: hier: Wörterbuch*
3. *subject: Schulfach*
4. *gym/gymnasium: Turnhalle*

Tom is a (0) <u>student</u> at a high school in Boston. Every morning he checks his (1) <u>school bag/satchel/schedule</u> to see if he has everything he needs: his books, his calculator and his pencil case. As he is doing a Spanish test today, Tom has to take his (2) <u>dictionary</u> to look up the words he doesn't know. He likes biology and English very much, but his favorite (3) <u>subject</u> is sports. In summer students use the sports fields but in winter they do sport in the (4) gy<u>m</u>/gy<u>mnasium</u>.

Aufgabe 3

Hinweis: *Hier werden deine Grammatikkenntnisse geprüft. Setze die vorgegebenen Verben in die richtige Zeitform. Beachte die Signalwörter, um die richtige Zeitform zu erkennen.*

	Signalwort	Zeit	Besonderheit
1	two weeks ago	simple past	„began" = unregelmäßiges Verb
2	two weeks ago	simple past	I, <u>he</u>, <u>she</u>, <u>it</u> wasn't
3	„isn't having" zeigt an, dass die Zeitebene nun wieder die Gegenwart ist	simple present	Während „isn't having" die Verlaufsform der Gegenwart darstellt, muss in die Lücke die Form des simple present („is").
4	every Saturday	simple present	he, she, it work<u>s</u>
5	for over a year now	present perfect	<u>he</u>, <u>she</u>, <u>it</u> ha<u>s</u>
6	if/next year (if-Satz Typ I)	will-future	Statt „will (buy)" ist im if-Satz auch die Verwendung von „can (buy)" möglich.

As everybody (0) <u>knows</u>, driving a car is very important in the USA. In some states people can get a driving license when they are 16. About two weeks ago Steven (1) <u>began</u> learning how to drive. The first lesson (2) <u>wasn't</u> easy. He isn't having lessons at a driving school because his father (3) <u>is</u> his instructor. Every Saturday Steven (4) <u>works</u> at a local supermarket. He (5) <u>has had</u> the job for over a year now. If he saves enough money, he (6) <u>will buy/can buy</u> himself a decent second-hand car next year.

Aufgabe 4

Hinweis: *Bei dieser Aufgabe geht es darum, dass du dich in Alltagssituationen angemessen ausdrücken kannst. Lies dir zunächst die Antwortsätze durch, damit du weißt, <u>wonach</u> du fragen sollst. Manchmal kannst du das Verb (z. B. ask, start) des Antwortsatzes auch für deine Frage verwenden. Beachte bei deinen Fragen die Umschreibung mit „to do": (evtl. Fragewort) + do (can, may ...) + you + Verb ...?*

Tim:	Can you help me, please? I have to give a talk about American schools.
Jill:	Of course, I can help you.
Tim:	<u>May I</u>/<u>Can I</u>/<u>Could I ask you</u> some questions?
Jill:	Sure. Just feel free to ask.
Tim:	<u>When do you start (school)</u>/<u>When does school start</u> in the morning?
Jill:	We start at 9. But before that I meet my friends.
Tim:	<u>Where do you meet</u> them?
Jill:	In the school cafeteria. We have breakfast there.
Tim:	<u>Do you bring</u>/<u>eat</u>/<u>take</u>/<u>have</u> your own food?
Jill:	No we don't. We have to buy the food at the cafeteria.

C Reading Comprehension

Allgemeiner Hinweis: *Im Lesetext geht es um die beiden Töchter des amerikanischen Präsidenten Barack Obama.*

Nach dem ersten Lesen solltest du den Inhalt des Textes im Wesentlichen verstanden haben. Schlage nur diejenigen Wörter nach, die du unbedingt zum Verständnis benötigst. Bei der Bearbeitung der Aufgaben ist es nötig, dass du zunächst diejenigen Textstellen findest, auf die sich die Aufgaben beziehen, und diese nochmals konzentriert durchliest, ehe du die Lösungen aufschreibst.

Vokabelhinweise:

Z. 1: *in the public eye: im Auge der Öffentlichkeit, von vielen Menschen beobachtet*
Z. 9: *incredible: unglaublich*
Z. 20: *to yawn: gähnen*
Z. 21 f.: *to remind: erinnern an*
Z. 23: *environment: hier: Umgebung, Umfeld*
Z. 25: *staff: Belegschaft, Mitarbeiter*
Z. 29: *responsibility: Verantwortung*
Z. 32: *college: Hochschule*
Z. 37: *to be proud of sb./sth.: stolz sein auf jmd./etw.*
Z. 40 f.: *to have a sleepover: bei jemanden übernachten*
Z. 44: *to deserve sth.: etw. verdienen*
Kasten: *rule: Regel*

Aufgabe 1

Hinweis: *Wenn du die Überschriften richtig zuordnest, zeigt dies, dass du den Inhalt des Textes im Wesentlichen verstanden hast.*
Vokabel: chores = Hausarbeit

paragraph 1 (lines 1–4)	C
paragraph 2 (lines 5–10)	G
paragraph 3 (lines 11–20)	A
paragraph 4 (lines 21–32)	B
paragraph 5 (lines 33–38)	E
paragraph 6 (lines 39–44)	F

Aufgabe 2

Hinweis: *Für jede Lücke ergibt nur jeweils ein Auswahl-Satz im Textzusammenhang einen Sinn. Beachte, dass ein Satz in keine Lücke passt.*

(0)	(1)	(2)	(3)	(4)	(5)
C	G	D	F	B	A

Aufgabe 3

Hinweis: *Beantworte die Fragen in Stichpunkten, indem du die Schlüsselwörter dem Lesetext entnimmst.*

1. Air Force One
   Hinweis: *Z. 5 f.; gefragt wird nach dem Namen des Flugzeugs des US-Präsidenten ("What <u>is</u> the President's aircraft <u>called</u>?").*

2. (on/at the) weekend
   Hinweis: *siehe Kasten, Absatz „Technology"; gefragt wird, wann die Töchter das Internet nutzen dürfen („allowed to use").*

3. make (their own) beds/set the table/take (the) dogs for a walk
   Hinweis: *Z. 26 ff.*

4. (have) sleepovers/(go to) shopping (mall)/(go to the) movies
   Hinweis: *Z. 40 f.*

Aufgabe 4

Hinweis: *Suche nach der Stelle im Lesetext, die in der jeweiligen Frage umschrieben wird und notiere dann den (Teil)Satz als Lösung.*

1. They have met lots of well-known people ...
   Hinweis: Z. 6 f. (celebrities: Stars, Berühmtheiten)
2. ... they have to listen and smile.
   Hinweis: Z. 18 f. (in public: in der Öffentlichkeit, vor anderen Leuten)
3. ... they're not going to be in the White House for ever. /
   Not long from now they'll be at college by themselves.
   Hinweis: Z. 30 ff. (present: gegenwärtig, momentan)
4. ... they have to write reports about what they saw ...
   Hinweis: Kasten, Absatz „Trips"
5. ... he is extremely proud of his children. / They're smart ... /
   ... they're respectful. / I could not have asked for better kids.
   Hinweis: Z. 37 f. (opinion: Meinung)
6. I've got tough guys with guns looking after my daughters.
   Hinweis: Z. 43 f. (well protected: gut behütet)

D Text Production

Allgemeiner Hinweis: *Entscheide dich <u>entweder</u> für die E-Mail <u>oder</u> für die Bildergeschichte. Du darfst ein zweisprachiges Wörterbuch verwenden. Beachte die Vorgaben zu Umfang, Form und Inhalt, die in der Aufgabenstellung beschrieben sind. Die Lösungsbeispiele sind jedoch bewusst etwas länger gehalten, so dass du verschiedene Ideen für deine eigene Lösung bekommst.*

1. Correspondence: E-Mail

Hinweis: *Lies dir die vorgegebene E-Mail gut durch. Du findest hier Fragen und Aufforderungen, auf die du in deiner Antwortmail eingehen sollst – du kannst aber auch eigene Ideen einbringen. Die Mail enthält viele Vokabeln und Ausdrücke, die du auch in deiner Antwort verwenden kannst. Da du das Job-Angebot annehmen möchtest, sollte deine Mail in einem höflichen und interessierten Ton geschrieben sein. Sie sollte neben dem Hauptteil auch eine Anrede (Dear/Hello Susan ...), einen Schlusssatz (Looking forward to hearing from you, See you in San Francisco ...), deinen Gruß (Best wishes, Take care ...) und deinen Namen enthalten. Der Inhalt sollte klar verständlich sein. Dabei spielen neben Ausdruck und Grammatik auch die Rechtschreibung und eine saubere äußere Form eine Rolle.*

Hello Susan,

Thanks for your e-mail! It was fantastic to hear from you because I was actually looking for a summer job when I got your mail. I would be happy to come to San Francisco and look after Justin!

My holidays are from August 1st until mid-September and I could stay with you the whole time. I hope that's OK with you.

I have to admit that I don't have much experience of working with children. I only have two older sisters and Aunt Emma's sons are also older than me. But one of my hobbies is playing soccer and I could teach Justin to play! Does Justin play soccer?

Do you live in a house with a garden, or in a flat?

I think that my English is quite good. I've been learning it at school for four years. Every time I visit aunt Emma, I speak English with her, too.

How much free time I will have during my stay? Do you think that I could do a surfing course?

I'm really looking forward to hearing from you!

Best wishes,
(your name)

2. Creative Writing: Picture-based Story

Hinweis: *Sieh dir zunächst die einzelnen Bilder genau an und versuche die Geschichte im Ganzen zu verstehen. Finde dabei die Pointe heraus (der Tintenfisch hat die Brille des Großvaters auf). Auch die Überschrift ("The big catch" – „Der große Fang") hilft dir beim Verständnis der Geschichte.*

Die Überschrift sowie der Einleitungssatz für den ersten Teil (Last summer ...) und den zweiten Teil (The next day ...) sind bereits vorgegeben. Du kannst diese in deine Geschichte übernehmen. Denke daran, deinen Text durch Absätze zu gliedern. Runde deine Geschichte mit einem geeigneten Schluss ab.

Deine Geschichte sollte auch für jemanden verständlich sein, der die zugehörigen Bilder nicht kennt. Du darfst also keine wichtigen Informationen auslassen. Achte außerdem auf Wortschatz, Grammatik und Rechtschreibung. Wörtliche Rede macht deine Geschichte lebendig!

The big catch

Last summer, Steve and his granddad were at the seaside. One sunny day, when they went fishing in a small boat, a stupid thing happened to Steve's grandpa. "There's a fish on my rod!" Steve's grandpa shouted excitedly, but while he was leaning over the boat to pull the fish out of the water, his glasses fell into the sea and were gone. Grandpa was very sad.

The next day Steve went fishing again, but this time he was on his own, so he just went fishing off a jetty. All of a sudden some other anglers yelled, "An octopus!" Steve felt there was something really heavy at the other end of his rod. It was a big octopus! Steve pulled it out onto the jetty. The craziest thing was that the octopus was wearing glasses, and that they were definitely grandpa's glasses! "What a big catch!" Steve thought when he carried the octopus and the glasses back home to his grandpa.

Steve's grandpa was very surprised to see Steve's catch. "Nobody will believe this story," he murmured with relief.

Notenschlüssel

Notenstufen	1	2	3	4	5	6
Punkte	80–68	67–55	54–41	40–27	26–13	12–0

Qualifizierender Abschluss der Mittelschule Bayern 2015
Lösungen – Englisch

A Listening

Allgemeiner Hinweis: *Der Hörverstehenstest besteht aus vier Teilen. Zu jedem Text, den du von der CD hörst, gibt es eine Aufgabe („Task"), die du mithilfe der Informationen aus dem jeweiligen Hörtext bearbeiten sollst.*
Verschaffe dir zuerst einen Überblick über die Aufgaben. Du hörst die Texte je zwei Mal ohne Unterbrechungen und Erläuterungen. Die Aufgaben kannst du entweder während des Zuhörens und/oder im Anschluss daran bearbeiten. In der Musterlösung sind teilweise mehrere Antwortmöglichkeiten angegeben. Du musst aber natürlich nur eine (richtige) Lösung aufschreiben.

Part 1

1   MARTIN: Hello. Um, I'd like a single to Aberdeen, please.
    TICKETSELLER: OK. Leaving today?
    MARTIN: If possible, yes. I think there's one that goes at ten past nine.
    TICKETSELLER: Yes, that's right but I'm afraid there's a short delay today because of
5   heavy traffic on the M4 coming in to London.
    MARTIN: Oh. OK.
    TICKETSELLER: At the moment we're looking at about 15 minutes. So it'll be just
        before nine thirty before you get away.
    MARTIN: That's fine. I've got a coach card.
10 TICKETSELLER: OK. Let's have a look. Right. Have you got any additional luggage?
    MARTIN: No, just this one bag.
    TICKETSELLER: OK. That's ... er ... £42.50.
    MARTIN: Oh, wow. So much? Even with a coach card?
    TICKETSELLER: Well, the 'walk-up' fares are always the most expensive. That
15   means if you want to leave right away, you'll have to pay more. But do you
        have to go today? Because if you book in advance, it's much cheaper.
    MARTIN: Oh. OK. No, I'm not in a rush.
    TICKETSELLER: Well, if you wait a day or two and book online, you can probably
        save another 30 per cent.
20 MARTIN: OK. Thanks. I can leave tomorrow. Thank you very much for your
        help ...

1. (at) **ten past nine/9.10**
   Hinweis: Z. 3

2. (because of) (heavy) **traffic**
   Hinweis: Z. 4 f.
3. (just before) **9.30**/(about) **15 min**(utes) **later**/(at) **9.25**
   Hinweis: Z. 7 f.
4. (just) **one** (piece/bag)
   Hinweis: Z. 10 f.
5. (£) **42.50**
   Hinweis: Z. 12
6. (another) **30 per cent/30 %**
   Hinweis: Z. 18 f.

Part 2

1 COACH DRIVER: Good morning. I'm John, your driver today. Before we leave, I'd like to apologise for our late departure from London this morning. We're about 20 minutes late at the moment but if everything goes well we should be able to make that up by around lunchtime.
5 I'd also like to apologise for some problems we're experiencing on this coach at the moment. As you can tell, it's very warm in here and that's because the air conditioning's not working properly. There's also a problem with the Wi-Fi and that's why there's no Internet available. However, we do have some good news. When we get to Luton there's going to be a change of driver but
10 we're also going to change the coach. So after Luton everything should be back to normal again.
Finally, I'd like to remind you to fasten your safety belts and to make sure your luggage is not blocking the aisle.
So, let's get on the way. Relax and enjoy the view. Thank you.
15 If you have any questions, please …

Hinweis: *Jeder in dieser Aufgabe vorgegebene Satz enthält einen inhaltlichen Fehler. Folge dem Text also aufmerksam und finde das Wort im Satz, das nicht mit dem Hörtext übereinstimmt. Schreibe das richtige Wort aus dem Hörtext auf.*

1. We're about ~~half an hour~~ late.
   20 minutes
   Hinweis: Z. 2 f.

2. We ~~won't~~ be able to make that up by around lunchtime.
   should
   ✏ Hinweis: Z. 3 f.
3. The ~~heating~~'s not working properly.
   air conditioning
   ✏ Hinweis: Z. 6 f.
4. There's no ~~on-board service~~ available.
   Internet/Wi-Fi
   ✏ Hinweis: Z. 7 f.
5. There's going to be a change of ~~tyres~~.
   driver/coach
   ✏ Hinweis: Z. 9 f.

Part 3

1   MARTIN: And are you going to Aberdeen, too?
    TOURIST: No, I'm getting out in Edinburgh.
    MARTIN: OK.
    TOURIST: Yeah, a friend of mine lives there and has invited me to stay with him.
5   Actually, he lives in a small place about half an hour from Edinburgh. What
        about you?
    MARTIN: I'm planning to go all the way to Aberdeen. I was thinking of going to
        the Highland Games on Saturday.
    TOURIST: Really? In Aberdeen? Have you got somewhere to stay?
10 MARTIN: No. I was thinking of trying the youth hostel there.
    TOURIST: Oh, I don't think you'll get a place there. Not now. The Games are very
        popular and everywhere will be booked out.
    MARTIN: OK. Have you got an idea what I could do?
    TOURIST: Well, the best thing would be to get a tent and go camping. I know a
15   campsite near Aberdeen. It's close to the river.
    MARTIN: Um, I'd need a sleeping bag, too.
    TOURIST: I know. But what about staying in a village close to Aberdeen? I know a
        place called Stonehaven. From there you can get a train to Aberdeen. It takes
        about 15 minutes. In fact I know a fantastic bed and breakfast place there.
20   Beachview. I can give you the website: beachview dot co dot uk.
    MARTIN: Sounds perfect. I'll write it down. What was it again?
    TOURIST: Beachview dot co dot uk.
    MARTIN: Thanks. As soon as we have access to the Internet I'll have a look at it …

1. The American tourist is staying with a **friend** near Edinburgh.
   Hinweis: Z. 4
2. The American thinks the youth hostels in Aberdeen will be **booked out/full**.
   Hinweis: Z. 11 f.
3. Martin would need a **tent/sleeping bag** for camping.
   Hinweis: Z. 14 ff.
4. Stonehaven is a **village/place** close to Aberdeen.
   Hinweis: Z. 17 f.
5. In Stonehaven Martin could stay at a **bed and breakfast** (place)/**B and B/B & B/B + B**.
   Hinweis: Z. 19

Part 4

GUIDE: Well, I think you know about the bagpiping competition. There are massed band competitions but there are solo piping competitions as well. But here are four more competitions I'd like to tell you about.
The first competition is the weight throw. The weights are made of metal. There's a chain with a handle on the end attached to the weight. The winner is the person who throws the weight the greatest distance, using one hand only.
The second competition is called "sheaf toss". A "sheaf" is a sack full of straw. It weighs about 10 kilos. To "toss" means to throw, but you don't throw the sack of straw as far as you can, you throw it up and over a bar. Not with your hands. You have to use a pitchfork!
The third competition is "tossing the caber". A caber is a tree trunk. It's about 5 metres long. You hold the caber at the bottom and toss it, or throw it, so it turns over in the air and lands on the ground. Of course, the heavier the caber the harder it is to throw it into the air.
A final competition I can tell you about is called "tug of war". Two teams stand at different ends of a long rope and pull as hard as they can. The team that pulls the other team four metres off the middle is the winner.
Of course there are other …

Hinweis: *Sieh dir bei jeder Aufgabe die Bilderfolge genau an, denn die Bilder unterscheiden sich nur in Einzelheiten. Damit du das richtige Bild findest, solltest du beim Hörtext auch auf feine Unterschiede achten, z.B. ob das Wurfgeschoss mit einer oder aber mit beiden Händen gehalten wird.*

1. Weight throw

   Hinweis: Z. 4 ff.

2. Sheaf toss

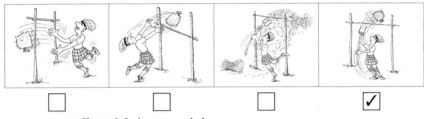

   Hinweis: Z. 7 ff.; pitchfork = Heugabel

3. Tossing the caber

   Hinweis: Z. 11 ff.

4. Tug of war

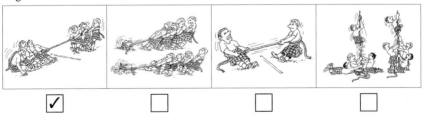

   Hinweis: Z. 15 ff.

B Use of English

Allgemeiner Hinweis: *In diesem Prüfungsteil musst du dein Wissen im Bereich Wortschatz, Grammatik und Rechtschreibung unter Beweis stellen.*

Aufgabe 1

Hinweis: *Diese Aufgabe testet deinen Wortschatz und deine Grammatikkenntnisse. Achte auch auf die korrekte Rechtschreibung der gesuchten Wörter.*
Lücke:
(1) „more than" = „mehr als"
(4) „to be famous for" = „berühmt sein für"
(5) Hier kannst du entweder das modale Hilfsverb „can" einsetzen oder auch das „will-future" verwenden.
(6) Frage mit „to be" im „simple present": "Are you interested in ...?" = „Bist du/ Sind Sie an ... interessiert?"

Scotland is (0) **part** of the United Kingdom. More (1) **than** five million people live there. Edinburgh, its capital, is the second largest (2) **city/town**. Aberdeen is called Europe's oil capital (3) **because/as/since/for** Scotland has the largest oil reserves in the European Union. Scotland is famous (4) **for** its lakes and mountains. All year round you (5) **can/will** find lots of tourists travelling the country. So, (6) **are** you interested in visiting Scotland?

Aufgabe 2

Hinweis: *Hier werden verschiedene Grammatikbereiche überprüft, z. B. die Bildung der Zeiten und die Steigerung von Adjektiven. Bei größeren Unsicherheiten empfiehlt sich die Wiederholung des jeweiligen Themas mithilfe der Kurzgrammatik, die du im Trainingsband findest.*
(1) Steigerung des Adjektivs „big": big – bigger – biggest. Beachte auch die Mitlautverdopplung „big/biggest".
(2) countries: Mehrzahl des Nomens „country". Achte auf die Rechtschreibung: aus „-y" wird „-ie".
(3) „went": Zeitform „simple past"; Signalwort „last August"
(4) „didn't stay": Zeitform „simple past", bezieht sich auch auf „last August"; hier ist das Verb zusätzlich verneint: „did not/didn't"
(5) „getting": die „ing"-Form folgt nach „like", wenn man etwas allgemein gerne tut.

(6) *Aufgrund des Signalworts „next year" muss hier eine Form stehen, die ein zukünftiges Ereignis ausdrückt; in diesem Fall kannst du sowohl das „will-future" als auch das „going-to future" oder das „present progressive" verwenden.*

Thousands of (0 tourist) **tourists** go to Edinburgh every year to experience the Festival. The Edinburgh Festival is one of the (1 big) **biggest** events in Scotland. People from Scotland and many other (2 country) **countries** go there. Last August Tim (3 go) **went** there for the first time. He (4 not stay) **didn't stay** long but he enjoyed it. Tim likes (5 get) **getting** to know different cultures. That's why he (6 fly) **will fly/is going to fly/is flying** to the USA next year.

Aufgabe 3

Hinweis: Hier werden dein Wortschatz und v. a. deine Grammatikkenntnisse getestet. Jede Aufgabe lenkt dein Augenmerk auf vier unterstrichene Stellen im Satz, wovon eine Stelle fehlerhaft ist. Den sprachlichen Fehler gilt es zu entdecken und zu markieren. Es wird nicht erwartet, dass du den Fehler erklärst oder berichtigst. Solltest du bei dieser Aufgabe Schwierigkeiten haben, empfiehlt sich ein Blick in die Kurzgrammatik des Trainingsbandes.

1. On Monday I climbed Ben Nevis, the most high mountain in Great Britain.
     A   B   Ⓒ   D

   Hinweis: Fehler bei der Steigerung des Adjektivs „high". Da es sich um ein einsilbiges Adjektiv handelt, lautet die richtige Steigerung „highest". (vgl. die Kurzgrammatik im Trainingsband, Kapitel 12)

2. On the way down I fell and ruined my jeans but I didn't hurt me.
               A B   C   Ⓓ

   Hinweis: Fehler bei der Auswahl des Fürwortes (Pronomens). Die richtige Lösung ist das rückbezügliche Fürwort „myself" (vgl. Kurzgrammatik, Kapitel 3).

3. The next day I met a man which showed me how to play the bagpipes.
     A   B   Ⓒ   D

   Hinweis: Fehler bei der Wahl des Relativpronomens. Die richtige Lösung lautet „who", weil hier auf eine Person („a man") Bezug genommen wird (vgl. Kurzgrammatik, Kapitel 11).

4. The weather has been really good so far: sunny and warm all time.
     A   B   C   Ⓓ

   Hinweis: Hier müsste es richtig heißen: „all of the time"

5. The best thing is: I <u>haven't met</u> <u>some</u> unfriendly <u>people</u>. <u>Everybody</u> is nice.
                                 A   Ⓑ   C   D

   Hinweis: *Fehler bei der Verwendung von „some/any". Da der Satz durch „haven't" verneint ist, muss <u>„any"</u> verwendet werden. „Some" verwendet man in bejahten Sätzen.*

6. If they speak <u>slow</u>, I <u>can</u> even understand <u>their</u> Scottish <u>accent</u>.
                       Ⓐ   B   C   D

   Hinweis: *Fehler bei der Unterscheidung von Adverb und Adjektiv. In diesem Satz wird das Adverb „slowly" benötigt, da das Verb „speak" näher beschrieben wird: <u>Auf welche Art und Weise</u> sprechen sie?*

7. At the moment I'm <u>at</u> the railway station. <u>I'm waiting of</u> my train <u>to</u> Edinburgh.
                              A   B   Ⓒ   D

   Hinweis: *Richtig ist die Wortverbindung „waiting <u>for</u>" für „warten <u>auf</u>".*

8. <u>I'm looking forward</u> <u>to</u> Edinburgh. <u>There are</u> so <u>much</u> things to see there!
      A   B   C   Ⓓ

   Hinweis: *Fehler bei der Unterscheidung von „much/many". Man verwendet hier <u>„many"</u>, weil das Namenwort (Nomen) „things" zählbar ist. Dies erkennst du daran, dass es von „thing" auch die Mehrzahlform („thing<u>s</u>") gibt. „Much" verwendet man bei Nomen, die <u>nicht</u> zählbar sind und somit auch keine Mehrzahlform haben, z. B. „much money".*

C Reading Comprehension

Allgemeiner Hinweis: *Nach dem ersten Lesen solltest du den Inhalt des Textes im Wesentlichen verstanden haben. Bei der Bearbeitung der Aufgaben ist es nötig, dass du zunächst diejenigen Textstellen findest, auf die sich die Aufgaben beziehen. Lies diese noch einmal durch, bevor du die Lösungen aufschreibst. Die folgende Vokabelliste ist bewusst umfangreich gehalten. In der Prüfung solltest du aus Zeitgründen aber nur die Wörter nachschlagen, die du zum Verständnis des Textes unbedingt brauchst.*

Vokabelhinweise:

Z. 1: *to take part in:* teilnehmen an
Z. 1 f.: *practice session:* Übungseinheit, Trainingseinheit
Z. 4: *to race:* hier: ein Rennen fahren
Z. 6: *profession:* Beruf
Z. 6: *dominated by:* dominiert, beherrscht von
Z. 8: *competitive:* leistungsorientiert, immer der/die Beste sein wollend
Z. 10: *to realise:* begreifen, erkennen
Z. 16: *championship:* Meisterschaft

Z. 20: *close links to:* enge Verbindungen zu
Z. 21: *development driver:* Testfahrer/in
Z. 23: *to be in a rush:* in Eile sein
Z. 25: *skill:* Fähigkeit, Fertigkeit
Z. 26: *physical strength:* körperliche Kraft
Z. 26 f.: *tight corners:* enge Kurven
Z. 27: *at high speeds:* bei hoher Geschwindigkeit
Z. 28: *to compete with sb:* gegen jmd. antreten, mit jmd. konkurrieren
Z. 32: *engineer:* Ingenieur/in
Z. 32: *equipment:* Ausrüstung
Z. 34: *to be scared:* Angst haben
Z. 37: *fear:* Angst
Z. 38: *failure:* Versagen
Z. 39: *impatient:* ungeduldig

Aufgabe 1

- **Hinweis:** Wenn du die Überschriften richtig zuordnest, zeigt dies, dass du den Inhalt des Textes im Wesentlichen verstanden hast.
- Vokabeln:
- *athletic:* athletisch, trainiert, fit
- *charity events:* Wohltätigkeitsveranstaltungen
- *race course:* Rennstrecke
- *successes:* Erfolge

paragraph 1 (lines 1–6)	B
paragraph 2 (lines 7–13)	D
paragraph 3 (lines 14–18)	F
paragraph 4 (lines 19–24)	G
paragraph 5 (lines 25–33)	A
paragraph 6 (lines 34–40)	E

Aufgabe 2

Hinweis: Diese Aufgabe überprüft das Detailverständnis, also wie genau du den Text verstanden hast. Lies zunächst jede Frage gut durch und schlage unbekannte Wörter nach, falls sie für das Verständnis wichtig sind. Markiere nun im Lesetext die Stelle, die die Antwort auf die jeweilige Frage beinhaltet. Notiere dann die Lösung. Es reicht, wenn du die Antwort knapp formulierst („short answers"), du kannst aber auch einen ganzen Satz schreiben. Wenn du einen Satz aus dem Text abschreibst, wähle nur die zur Frage passenden Stellen aus und passe den Satzbau entsprechend der Frage an.

1. in her teens
   Hinweis: Z. 10 f.; when = wann, unusual = ungewöhnlich
2. (they met) in her dad's (motorbike) shop
   Hinweis: Z. 12 f.; how = wie, to get to know each other = sich kennenlernen
3. (her) husband/Toto Wolff
   Hinweis: Z. 19 f.; who = wer, connections = Kontakte, Verbindungen
4. head and neck
   Hinweis: Z. 26 ff.; which = hier: welche (Körperteile), pressure = Druck
5. She's careful about what she eats. / She trains for two hours every day.
   Hinweis: Z. 30 f.; what = was, in order to = um ... zu

Aufgabe 3

Hinweis: Diese Aufgabe ist etwas anspruchsvoller, da du dir die Antworten erschließen musst; du findest sie nicht wörtlich im Text. Es ist wichtig, dass du den Inhalt der vorgegebenen Sätze genau verstehst – schlage also unbekannte Wörter im Wörterbuch nach. Suche dann die inhaltsgleichen Abschnitte im Lesetext und notiere die Fundstelle (Zeilenangaben).

	line or lines
1.	8
2.	15/16
3.	22/23
4.	25/26
5.	35/36

Aufgabe 4

Hinweis: *Bei dieser Aufgabe werden dir englische Wörter vorgegeben, die im Text vorkommen, sowie jeweils vier verschiedene Möglichkeiten, das Wort ins Deutsche zu übersetzen. Die Angaben in Klammern sind grammatikalische Zusatzinformationen, die dir helfen können, die richtige Antwort zu finden. Lies dir zunächst im Lesetext den gesamten Satz durch, der das betreffende Wort enthält. Nun hast du verschiedene Möglichkeiten vorzugehen:*
Übersetze den Satz aus dem Text ins Deutsche und kreuze das richtige Wort an oder setze jedes angegebene deutsche Wort für das englische Wort in den Text ein. Beim Übersetzen wirst du schnell herausfinden, ob die jeweilige Bedeutung im Satzzusammenhang einen Sinn ergibt oder nicht.

1. time (line 4)
   - [ ] Zeit *(Nomen)*
   - [✓] Mal *(Nomen)*
   - [ ] stoppen *(Verb + Obj.)*
   - [ ] einen geeigneten Zeitpunkt wählen *(Verb + Obj.)*

   Hinweis: *Das letzte Mal, dass dies eine Frau tat, war 1975, als Lella Lombardi, eine italienische Fahrerin, in Südafrika ein Rennen fuhr.*

2. turn (line 22)
   - [ ] wenden, umdrehen *(Verb + Obj.)*
   - [ ] abbiegen *(Verb)*
   - [✓] werden *(Verb ohne Obj.)*
   - [ ] Kurve, Biegung *(Nomen)*

   Hinweis: *Im Dezember dieses Jahres wird Susie 33 Jahre alt.*

3. mean (line 26)
   - [✓] bedeuten *(Verb + Obj.)*
   - [ ] meinen *(Verb)*
   - [ ] geizig *(Adj.)*
   - [ ] gemein *(Adj.)*

   Hinweis: *Was bedeutet das für einen Rennfahrer/eine Rennfahrerin?*

4. light (line 31)
   - [ ] Licht *(Nomen)*
   - [ ] anzünden *(Verb + Obj.)*
   - [ ] erleuchten *(Verb + Obj.)*
   - [x] leicht *(Adj.)*

   Hinweis: Sie ist klein und <u>leicht</u>, und in der Formel 1 ist das von Vorteil.

5. like (line 35)
   - [ ] mögen *(Verb + Obj.)*
   - [ ] möchten *(Verb + Obj.)*
   - [x] wie *(Präp.)*
   - [ ] also *(Adv.) (umgs)*

   Hinweis: <u>Wie</u> alle Formel 1-Fahrer kennt sie die Risiken.

D Text Production

Allgemeiner Hinweis: *Entscheide dich <u>entweder</u> für die E-Mail <u>oder</u> für die Bildergeschichte. Du darfst ein zweisprachiges Wörterbuch verwenden. Beachte die Vorgaben zu Umfang, Form und Inhalt, die in der Aufgabenstellung beschrieben sind. Die Lösungsbeispiele sind bewusst etwas länger gehalten, sodass du verschiedene Ideen für deine eigene Lösung bekommst.*

1. Correspondence: E-Mail

Hinweis: *Lies dir die Aufgabenstellung genau durch und versetze dich in die beschriebene Situation. Bei Alex handelt es sich vermutlich um einen etwa gleichaltrigen Schüler/eine gleichaltrige Schülerin, zu dem/der du im Rahmen eines Austauschprogramms einen ersten Kontakt herstellen möchtest. Du schreibst also eine persönliche E-Mail, die mit keinen besonderen Anforderungen an die Form verbunden ist (wie das z.B. bei einer Bewerbung nötig wäre). Vergiss dennoch nicht, eine Anrede und eine passende Verabschiedung mit Angabe deines Namens einzufügen. Gehe in deiner E-Mail auf die Punkte ein, die in der Aufgabenstellung angegeben sind. Manchmal kannst du auch auswählen oder selbst entscheiden, über was du in deiner E-Mail schreiben möchtest. Gehe aber auf jeden Fall auf alle geforderten Punkte der Reihe nach ein.*

Hi Alex,

How are you? I'm writing to introduce myself. My name is Michael and I'm in the ninth grade of your German partner school. I'm really looking forward to visiting you in July! I think it will be interesting to meet you and be at your school – and it will be great to practise my English.

Do you do a lot of sports at your school? That would be great because I'm quite a sporty guy. I love playing football and tennis.

How many kids are in our class? What do you usually do in your free time?

I hope there will be time to visit some places in Scotland – do you think we could go to Loch Ness together? Or are there other places you would suggest? Do you have any ideas what we could do in the evenings?

I also wanted to ask if I will have my own room while I'm staying at your place.

Before I forget it, I wanted to tell you that I have a gluten allergy, which means that I can only eat bread or pasta that is gluten-free, but I eat all other foods.

I hope you are fine and I'm looking forward to hearing from you!

Best wishes, Michael *(209 words)*

2. Creative Writing: Picture Story

Hinweis: *In der Aufgabenstellung findest du bereits den Titel der Geschichte ("The Scottish castle ghost"), eine kurze Einleitung ("Last summer...") sowie fünf Bilder. Betrachte sie ganz genau, um den Inhalt der Geschichte zu verstehen. Überlege dir zu jedem Bild, was du dazu schreiben könntest und überlege dir Formulierungen auf Englisch. Beschreibe dann die Handlung der Geschichte von Bild zu Bild. Gliedere deinen Text in Absätze. Lies dir am Ende alles noch einmal durch: Ist deine Geschichte verständlich? Hast du den Witz der Geschichte erfasst (ein echtes Gespenst erscheint und Callum erschreckt sich selbst)?*

The Scottish castle ghost

Last summer Callum and his class visited an old Scottish castle. A friendly guide showed them suits of armour and pictures of people who had lived in the castle hundreds of years ago. While the other pupils were listening to the guide, Callum secretly pulled a ghost costume out of his bag and put it on. Then he shouted "Huuuuu" and waved his arms at his classmates. Everyone was terribly frightened and ran away.

"That trick really worked," Callum said to himself smiling. But he couldn't enjoy the moment for long because suddenly a real ghost appeared and Callum was completely shocked himself! Maybe the ghost wanted to teach Callum a lesson not to frighten other people. *(121 words)*

Notenschlüssel

Notenstufen	1	2	3	4	5	6
Punkte	80–68	67–55	54–41	40–27	26–13	12–0

Qualifizierender Abschluss der Mittelschule Bayern 2016
Lösungen – Englisch

A Listening

Allgemeiner Hinweis: *Es werden vier kurze Hörtexte von der CD vorgespielt. Dein Hörverständnis wird dann mittels der zugehörigen Aufgaben überprüft: Task 1 bezieht sich auf Part 1, Task 2 auf Part 2, usw. Lies die Aufgaben zuerst genau durch. So erkennst du, auf welche Informationen du dich beim Hören des jeweiligen Textes besonders konzentrieren solltest. Löse dann während des Zuhörens oder in der Pause im Anschluss die Aufgaben. Die Hörtexte werden zwei Mal vorgespielt. Im Prüfungsteil Listening Comprehension erhältst du für Rechtschreibfehler keinen Punktabzug, solange deine Lösung noch als inhaltlich richtig erkannt werden kann.*

Part 1

1 EMPLOYEE: Good afternoon, Stratford tourist office. Wendy Taylor speaking. How can I help you?
MR THOMPSON: Hello, Peter Thompson here. I'm going on a holiday in Europe later this year. My son and me, we're thinking about spending two or three
5 days in Stratford.
EMPLOYEE: That sounds great.
MR THOMPSON: Yes, ... well, ... you see, we're not sure if there's enough to see and do in Stratford if we stay that long.
EMPLOYEE: Well, since this is the anniversary year, there are even more events
10 than usual.
MR THOMPSON: Anniversary?
EMPLOYEE: Well, you know that Stratford is the hometown of William Shakespeare, the well-known playwright ...
MR THOMPSON: Of course I do.
15 EMPLOYEE: ... and he died in sixteen-hundred and sixteen, exactly 400 years ago.
MR THOMPSON: So are there any special events in Stratford this year?
EMPLOYEE: Unfortunately you missed the great parade on 23rd April, that's Shakespeare's birthday and also the day he died. But there are celebrations all year. And there are some special historical walks with a guide who explains
20 what the town was like in Shakespeare's time. And of course the usual sightseeing tours.
MR THOMPSON: Could you send me some information about the special anniversary events, please?

EMPLOYEE: Of course, but you can also find them on our website at shakespearean-
niversary.co.uk.
MR THOMPSON: Can I make reservations online, too?
EMPLOYEE: Yes, you will find booking forms on our website.
MR THOMPSON: OK. Thank you very much. You've been very helpful.
EMPLOYEE: You are welcome, Mr Thompson. Goodbye.
MR THOMPSON: Goodbye.

Hinweis: Finde in jedem Satz die falsche Information und ersetze diese durch die richtige Angabe aus dem Hörtext.

1. We're thinking about spending two or three ~~weeks~~ **days** in Stratford.
   Hinweis: Z. 5
2. There are even more ~~tourists~~ **events** than usual.
   Hinweis: Z. 9
3. William Shakespeare died in ~~1600~~ **1616**.
   Hinweis: Z. 15
4. You missed the great parade on ~~3rd~~ **23rd** April.
   Hinweis: Z. 17
5. Find them on our website at shakespeareanniversary.~~com~~ **co.uk**
   Hinweis: Z. 24 f.

Part 2

GUIDE: ... and we've already arrived at our next stop. Ladies and Gentlemen, the famous Royal Shakespeare Theatre! Here you can see many of Shakespeare's plays live on stage. The building you are looking at is actually about 70 years old. After some years of renovation it reopened again in 2010. In fact there are two theatres here.

The Royal Shakespeare Theatre has about 1,000 seats. And the Swan Theatre at the back of the building is about half that size.

The ticket counters are open for another hour today, so if you are interested in seeing a play, you can buy some tickets while we're here. Several different plays by Shakespeare are currently in the programme: Romeo and Juliet, Hamlet and A Midsummer Night's Dream.

Enjoy your time here. And don't forget, we move on at 4.30. The final stop of our tour is Holy Trinity Church. There, we'll visit Shakespeare's grave. *(fading)* And by the way, did you know that Shakespeare rarely ...

✏ **Hinweis:** *Achte auf die Informationen des Reiseführers im Hörtext, sodass du die richtigen Aussagen in Task 2 erkennst und in die Tabelle eintragen kannst.*
1. B (Z. 2f.)
2. D (Z. 4)
3. E (Z. 6f.; „half that size" = halb so groß)
4. I (Z. 13)

1	2	3	4
B	D	E	I

Part 3

1 MAN: Good afternoon. Can I help you?
   ROBERT: Good afternoon. I'm in Stratford this week and I'd like to see *Romeo and Juliet*. Are there any seats available?
   MAN: Let me see. Do you want to see an afternoon or an evening performance?
5 ROBERT: Evening, please.
   MAN: Well, Tuesday is fully booked and on the two following days we are showing *Hamlet*.
   ROBERT: Oh dear, and we leave an Friday.
   MAN: Well, there are seats for the afternoon performance on Wednesday at 4.15.
10 ROBERT: Yes, that would be OK.
   MAN: We have tickets in the circle for £ 25 and in the upper circle for £ 35 or £ 40.
   ROBERT: Oh, that's rather expensive.
   MAN: Well, how old are you?
15 ROBERT: I'm 16.
   MAN: Great, then we can offer you a discount ticket for £ 15.
   ROBERT: Fantastic. Can I book two tickets for the circle?
   MAN: Two tickets?
   ROBERT: Yes, I want to come with my father.
20 MAN: I see. He'll have to pay the full price, I'm afraid. That'll be £ 40 for the two of you.
   ROBERT: Yes, all right. Do I have to pay now?
   MAN: Either that or you can pick up your tickets on Wednesday and pay then. But you'll have to do that at least one hour before the performance starts.
25 ROBERT: That's fine.
   MAN: Then I will reserve the tickets for you … in the name of …?
   ROBERT: Thompson, Robert Thompson.

MAN: OK, two tickets are reserved for you in row D in the circle for the performance of *Romeo and Juliet* on Wednesday afternoon.
30 ROBERT: Thank you very much. Goodbye.
MAN: Goodbye.

Hinweis: *Ergänze die fehlenden Angaben im Formular.*

1. Wednesday
   Hinweis: *Z. 9*
2. 4.15 (pm)
   Hinweis: *Z. 9*
3. 1/one
   Hinweis: *Z. 16–20*
4. 40
   Hinweis: *Z. 20 f.*
5. one hour before (the performance/show starts) / 3.15 (pm)
   Hinweis: *Z. 23 f.*
6. D (in the circle)
   Hinweis: *Z. 28 f.*

Part 4

1 WAITRESS: Are you ready to order now?
MR THOMPSON: Well, not quite, I'm afraid.
WAITRESS: Perhaps I can get you something to drink?
MR THOMPSON: Yes, that's a good idea. What would you like to drink, Robert?
5 ROBERT: A coke, please.
WAITRESS: And for you, sir?
MR THOMPSON: I'd like some water, please.
WAITRESS: OK, thank you. I'll be right back.
MR THOMPSON: So, Robert, would you like to have a starter? How about the soup
10 of the day?
ROBERT: What sort of soup is it?
MR THOMPSON: Vegetable, I think.
ROBERT: Hmm, …
MR THOMPSON: Or would you prefer a tuna salad?
15 ROBERT: I think I'll have the Caesar's salad.
MR THOMPSON: Well, I'll go for the soup, I think. And what about a main course?
ROBERT: I don't really like fish.

MR THOMPSON: Well, the beef steak sounds very nice, doesn't it?
ROBERT: Only if it is well-done. Otherwise I'll take something else.
20 MR THOMPSON: We'll ask the waitress then. And which vegetables do you want to have?
ROBERT: I'll have the roast potatoes.
MR THOMPSON: It seems they've only got them baked or mashed.
ROBERT: Then I'll have mashed potatoes and carrots. And what about you?
25 MR THOMPSON: I'm having the grilled fish, baked potatoes and peas. And an apple pie for dessert.
ROBERT: And I'll have the toffee surprise rather than the lemon tart.
WAITRESS: Here are your drinks. A coke for you, ... and a mineral water for you, sir. Can I take your order now?
30 MR THOMPSON: Is the beef steak well-done?
WAITRESS: As you wish, you can have it well-done, if you like.
MR THOMPSON: Good, in that case we would like to have one well-done beef steak with ...

Hinweis: *In diesem Dialog erfährst du, was sich Robert (R) und sein Vater (F) als Vorspeise, Hauptgericht, Beilage und zum Nachtisch bestellen. Trage jeweils das Namenskürzel (R oder F) in die Kästchen ein.*

1. Ceasar's Salad   [R]
   Vegetable Soup   [F]
   Hinweis: *Robert: Z. 15, Father: Z. 16*

2. Grilled Fish   [F]
   Beef Steak   [R]
   Hinweis: *Robert: Z. 18 f./32, Father: Z. 25*

3. Baked Potatoes   [F]
   Mashed Potatoes   [R]
   Hinweis: *Robert: Z. 24, Father: Z. 25*

4. Carrots   [R]
   Peas   [F]
   Hinweis: *Robert: Z. 24, Father: Z. 25*

5. Apple Pie   [F]
   Toffee Surprise   [R]
   Hinweis: *Robert: Z. 27, Father: Z. 25 f.*

B Use of English

✒ **Allgemeiner Hinweis:** *In diesem Prüfungsteil musst du dein Wissen im Bereich Wortschatz, Grammatik und Rechtschreibung unter Beweis stellen.*

Aufgabe 1

✒ **Hinweis:** *Schreibe das Wort in der Klammer in der richtigen Form in die Lücke, sodass es sich korrekt in den vorgegebenen Satz einfügt. Anbei findest du eine Zuordnung der Lösungen zum jeweiligen Grammatikbereich. Solltest du bei der Bearbeitung dieser Aufgabe Schwierigkeiten gehabt haben, empfiehlt es sich, das jeweilige Grammatikthema nochmals in der Kurzgrammatik zu wiederholen.*

1 most important: Steigerung und Vergleich
2 don't have/haven't had: Zeiten (Simple present/Present perfect)
3 does: Zeiten/Fragen mit to do-Umschreibung im Simple present
4 includes: Zeiten (Simple present)
5 healthy/healthier: Adjektive/Steigerung und Vergleich
6 (prefer) having/to have: -ing-Form oder Infinitiv nach bestimmten Verben
7 European: Adjektive Länder/Kontinente
8 has existed: Zeiten (Present perfect)
9 quickly: Adverbien der Art und Weise
10 will change/is going to change: Zeiten (Aussagen über die Zukunft)

People have different ideas and (0 opinion) **opinions** about breakfast. Some people say it is the (1 important) **most important** meal of the day. Statistics show that people who (2 not have) **don't have/haven't had** breakfast often have problems with concentration and health. England is known for its cooked breakfast; but what (3 do) **does** this full English breakfast consist of? A typical English breakfast (4 include) **includes** eggs, either poached or scrambled, with bacon and sausages, followed by toast with marmalade. A (5 health) **healthy/healthier** version is just one egg and some toast. Whereas in Europe, especially in Germany, people prefer (6 have) **having/to have** cheese, ham, eggs and some bread as a start to the day, nearly all the southern (7 Europe) **European** countries tend to have only coffee and some bread or pastries. The tradition of the English breakfast (8 exist) **has existed** for many years, and visitors, hotel guests and people who have the time still enjoy it to this day. However, in our hectic and health-conscious world, many English people prefer a continental breakfast or they (9 quick) **quickly** get something to eat and drink on their way to work. It is likely that in future our culture of eating (10 change) **will change/is going to change** even more. The full English breakfast may soon be a thing of the past.

Aufgabe 2

✏ **Hinweis:** *Bei dieser anspruchsvollen Aufgabe ist dir kein Wort vorgegeben, sondern du musst selbst ein Wort finden, das in den Satzzusammenhang passt.*

1 *from* China: *aus* China
2 in *every* street: in *jeder* Straße
3 to *put/pour*: geben, gießen
4 so that they *did/would* not break: damit sie nicht zerbrachen, zerbrechen würden
5 *at* 4 o'clock: *um* 4 Uhr
6 *others/some/many*: andere/einige/viele
7 *that/which*: hier Relativpronomen: die, welche
8 *have* closed (Present perfect): haben zugemacht
9 *for example/for instance*: zum Beispiel
10 *there is*: es gibt

Since the 18th (0) **century** the United Kingdom has been one of the world's greatest tea consumers. At first, tea was mainly imported (1) **from** China. In those days it was sold in almost (2) **every** street in London. People at that time called it 'China drink'. Not only tea but also small porcelain tea cups were shipped to Europe. These cups were so thin that it was necessary to (3) **put/pour** some milk in first, so that they (4) **did/would** not break when the hot tea went in. People still use these porcelain cups now and then for special occasions. Even today people in England add milk to their tea and some sugar, depending on their taste. In Britain the word 'tea' describes both a hot drink and a light meal in the afternoon (5) **at** about four o'clock. For some people it is their last meal of the day, for (6) **others/some/many** a snack between lunch and dinner. In many towns and cities in Britain there are tea rooms (7) **that/which** serve tea and other drinks. But since the 1950s many tea rooms (8) **have** closed. Today people prefer health-orientated drinks, for (9) **example/instance** fruit or herbal teas. Nevertheless, (10) **there** is no other country in Europe where people drink more tea.

C Reading Comprehension

✏ **Allgemeiner Hinweis:** *In diesem Prüfungsteil darfst du ein Wörterbuch (aber kein elektronisches) verwenden. Lies dir den Text durch und versuche ihn grob zu verstehen. Markiere auch unbekannte Wörter. Beim zweiten Durchgang sollte dein Ziel sein, den Text genau zu verstehen. Schlage hierzu die markierten Wörter im Wörterbuch nach, die du zum detaillierten Textverständnis benötigst. Beginne anschließend mit der Bearbeitung der Aufgaben. Verwende auch hier bei sprachlichen Unklarheiten das Wörterbuch, damit du die Aufgabenstellung verstehst.*

Vokabelhinweise:
Z. 1: *vinegar:* Essig
Z. 9: *deep-fried:* frittiert
Z. 9: *batter:* Panade
Z. 9: *flour:* Mehl
Z. 17: *rationed:* rationiert, nur in begrenzter Menge erhältlich
Z. 19: *filling:* hier: sättigend
Z. 22: *posh:* vornehm, fein
Z. 30: *nowadays:* heutzutage
Z. 32: *fake:* hier: nachgemacht, (einer Zeitung) nachempfunden
Z. 36: *valuable source:* wertvolle Quelle
Z. 39: *physically:* körperlich, hier auch: für den Körper
Z. 39: *mentally:* seelisch, hier auch: für die Seele
Kasten:
flour (self-raising): Mehl mit Backpulverzusatz
to boil: in Wasser kochen
to sprinkle: träufeln
ingredient: Zutat
bowl: Schüssel

Aufgabe 1

✏ **Hinweis:** *Der Lesetext ist in Absätze (paragraphs A–F) gegliedert. Ordne jedem dieser Absätze jeweils die passende Überschrift zu. Drei Überschriften stimmen inhaltlich nicht mit dem Lesetext überein.*

Vokabelhinweis:
occasion: Anlass

paragraph B	paragraph C	paragraph D	paragraph E	paragraph F
7	6	3	2	4

Aufgabe 2

🖊 **Hinweis:** *Beantworte die Fragen anhand des Lesetextes. Du kannst in Stichpunkten antworten.*

1. flour, salt, (sparkling) water, beer
   🖊 **Hinweis:** *Abschnitt B, im Kasten: "For the batter"*
2. (the) Spanish
   🖊 **Hinweis:** *Z. 12 f.*
3. (because it was) cheap (and) filling
   🖊 **Hinweis:** *Z. 17 ff.*
4. (it) kept (the) food warm
   🖊 **Hinweis:** *Z. 29 f.*
5. plastic
   🖊 **Hinweis:** *Z. 32 f.*

Aufgabe 3

🖊 **Hinweis:** *Hier musst du notieren, wo die angegebenen Informationen im Lesetext zu finden sind. Gib dabei jeweils die Zeilen an.*

	line or lines
1.	22–23
2.	25–26
3.	31–32
4.	34
5.	36

Aufgabe 4

🖊 **Hinweis:** *Von den Aussagen b–j decken sich nur fünf mit dem Inhalt des Lesetextes. Vergleiche die Aussagen mit den Informationen aus dem Lesetext, wähle die richtigen Aussagen aus und notiere diese.*

1. c
   🖊 **Hinweis:** *Z. 8 f., sowie Kasten vorletzte Zeile*

2. e
   ✐ **Hinweis:** *Abschnitt B, Kasten: vorletzte und letzte Zeile*
3. f
   ✐ **Hinweis:** *Z. 14 ff.*
4. i
   ✐ **Hinweis:** *Z. 23*
5. j
   ✐ **Hinweis:** *Z. 35 f.*

D Text Production

✐ **Allgemeiner Hinweis:** *Entscheide dich <u>entweder</u> für die E-Mail <u>oder</u> für die Bildergeschichte. Du darfst ein zweisprachiges Wörterbuch verwenden. Beachte die Vorgaben zu Umfang, Form und Inhalt. Die Lösungsbeispiele sind jedoch etwas länger gehalten, sodass du verschiedene Ideen für deine eigene Lösung bekommst.*

1. Correspondence: E-Mail

✐ **Hinweis:** *Schreibe eine E-Mail an Carmen <u>oder</u> José. Was den Inhalt deiner E-Mail betrifft, so erhältst du in der Aufgabe bereits fünf Vorgaben (mit • gekennzeichnet), auf die du unbedingt eingehen musst. Diese Vorgaben darfst du selbst ausgestalten – Ideen und Beispiele, was du jeweils schreiben könntest, findest du ebenfalls in den Angaben (mit – gekennzeichnet). Vergiss nicht, in deiner E-Mail eine Anrede, eine Schlussformel sowie deinen Namen einzufügen. Die folgende E-Mail ist ein Lösungsbeispiel.*

Dear Carmen,

How are you? I hope you're fine. I'm quite happy with my English course here in Malta. My parents said I should go there. They love Malta because they met there twenty years ago at a language course. The teachers and the students at the language school are nice, but most students are German. So it's a pity that I don't speak English a lot during after-class activities. Lessons are from 9 am to 1 pm every day, with only two short breaks. After a light lunch we go to the beach or we sometimes visit historic places. Have you ever done a language course before? I've got an idea: I'd like to do another language course next summer. Could you imagine joining me? How about Ireland? We could study together and also speak English in our free time.

Best wishes,

(your name)

(146 words)

2. Creative Writing: Picture Story

✏ Hinweis: *Schreibe die Bildergeschichte „A new job". Der Anfang ist bereits vorgegeben. Er ist in der Zeitform „Simple past" (Hinweis: „were") verfasst – behalte also diese Zeitform auch in deinem Text bei. Erzähle, was in jedem Bild passiert und verbinde diese Informationen zu einem schlüssigen Text. Beschriftungen (z. B. „Rocky Gorilla") oder Sprechblasen (z. B. „Help!!!") verdeutlichen zum einen die Bilder und dürfen außerdem von dir direkt in deine Geschichte, z. B. als wörtliche Rede, übernommen werden. Achte darauf, dass deine Geschichte in Einleitung, Hauptteil und Schluss gegliedert ist. Der folgende Text ist ein Lösungsbeispiel.*

A new job

One morning, Mr Smith, the zoo director, and Nick, the zookeeper, were in a panic. Rocky, the gorilla, had escaped!
The two men stood in front of Rocky's cage. They saw that the door was open, and they had no clue where Rocky could be. Mr Smith had an idea: Nick should wear a gorilla costume and replace Rocky. Nick didn't like the idea at all, but he didn't have a choice. Soon he was inside the costume and hanging in Rocky's tree. The visitors didn't notice anything, but silly Nick leaned too far into Leo Lion's place. The branch Nick was sitting on broke off and he fell on the floor, in front of Leo's feet, and screamed "Help!!!" Instead of attacking the gorilla, Leo Lion took off his head: It was Nick's colleague, wearing a lion's costume! He whispered: "Nick, Shhh...! Or they will fire us both!"
It looked like Mr Smith had had this idea before. But, where had the animals gone?

(169 words)

Notenschlüssel

Notenstufen	1	2	3	4	5	6
Punkte	80–68	67–55	54–41	40–27	26–13	12–0

| Qualifizierender Abschluss der Mittelschule Bayern 2017 |
| Lösungen – Englisch |

A Listening

Allgemeiner Hinweis: *In diesem Teil der Prüfung musst du Hörtexten Informationen entnehmen. Du hörst zuerst einen Dialog, in dem es um die Suche nach einem Ausbildungsplatz geht. Im zweiten Hörtext wird von einer Arbeitserfahrung in Australien berichtet. Der dritte Text ist ein Bewerbungsgespräch. Im vierten Hörtext folgst du einem Kundengespräch in einer Autowerkstatt.*
Jeder Hörtext wird zweimal vorgespielt. Du hast in den Pausen vor und nach den Texten ausreichend Zeit, um die Aufgabenstellungen durchzulesen bzw. die Lösungen einzutragen. Rechtschreibfehler führen nicht zu Punktverlust, solange deine Lösung inhaltlich richtig ist.

Part 1 – Aufgabe 1

1   KIM: Hello?
    UNCLE BOB: Hi, Kim. It's your uncle Bob. How are you getting on? Are you still looking for a job as a car mechanic?
    KIM: Yes, no luck so far, I'm afraid.
5   UNCLE BOB: Well, I've just seen an advert in the local newspaper. Brown's Garage is offering an apprenticeship. Are you interested?
    KIM: Hmm ... what qualifications are required?
    UNCLE BOB: Let me see ... You have to be at least 16 years old ... They want good grades in maths and physics ... It also says that some work experience would be
10 helpful, but it's not absolutely necessary. And you don't need a driving licence.
    KIM: Aha, OK. And do you know where Brown's Garage is?
    UNCLE BOB: Yes, it's not far from my house.
    KIM: Oh, so it's in Brighton? And you know them?
    UNCLE BOB: Yes, I've been taking my car there for years. They are very reliable, and
15 friendly, too.
    KIM: Oh, and how can I get in touch with them?
    UNCLE BOB: I suggest you contact David, he is the head mechanic. He will be able to give you more information about the job. He is an interesting guy. He used to work in Australia as a car mechanic for a while. He even has his own video
20 blog. I'll find the link and send it to you.
    KIM: Thanks, uncle Bob.
    UNCLE BOB: That's OK, bye.

Hinweis: Da die Reihenfolge der Teilaufgaben der Abfolge im Hörtext entspricht, kannst du die fehlenden Informationen der Reihe nach dem Gespräch entnehmen. Achte vor allem bei Aufgabe 5 auf die richtige Schreibung. Wenn du hier anstatt „*head* mechanic" „hat mechanic" schreibst, wird aus der richtigen Lösung „Kfz-Meister" (sozusagen der „*Chef*-Mechaniker") ein „Hut-Mechaniker", was natürlich keinen Sinn ergibt.

1. Kim could do an apprenticeship at **Brown's** Garage.
   Hinweis: Z. 5 f.
2. Kim must have good grades in **maths** and **physics**.
   Hinweis: Z. 8 f.
3. Kim doesn't need work experience or a **driving licence/driver's license/driver's licence**.
   Hinweis: Z. 9 f.
4. The garage is in **Brighton**.
   Hinweis: Z. 13 f.
5. David, the **head** mechanic, has more information about the job.
   Hinweis: Z. 17 f.; die Lösungen „hat" und „had" sind falsch.

Part 2 – Aufgabe 2

1   DAVID MCKINLEY: Hi everyone. My name is David McKinley. I'm from Brighton and I'm a car mechanic.
    I worked for a while in Australia as a mobile mechanic. People over there often live so far away that they don't have the time to take their car to the garage. They
5   want repairs on the spot.
    I had a truck with all my tools in it and I went where the work was. That was anything ... from doing a safety check in town to changing tyres on a van or fixing the brakes of a road train way out in the country.
    If I didn't have the parts I needed, I had to use what I had in the truck. I spent
10 whole nights working under broken-down trucks and more than once I was up to my knees in water trying to pull a jeep out of a swamp.
    People were always pleased to see me but in some cases I couldn't repair their vehicles. So I ended up towing them for miles to the next town.
    Did I like working there? Yes, sure. You just had to remember that there were
15 snakes and spiders everywhere, even in your car! Lots of variety, lots of surprises. But I met all kinds of people and made some friends for life.
    If you want to know more please feel free to contact me ...

✏ **Hinweis:** *Du findest hier eine Auflistung verschiedener Aussagen. Wähle die vier Aussagen aus, die sinngemäß im Hörtext vorkommen. Es ist egal, in welcher Reihenfolge du sie notierst.*

1. ✏ **Hinweis:** D – „repairs on the spot" (Z. 4 f.)
2. ✏ **Hinweis:** F – „whole nights" (Z. 9 f.)
3. ✏ **Hinweis:** G – „up to my knees in water" (Z. 10 f.)
4. ✏ **Hinweis:** I – „remember that there were snakes and spiders" (Z. 14 f.)

1	2	3	4
D	F	G	I

Part 3 – Aufgabe 3

1 MR BROWN: Good afternoon, Kim. I am Mr Brown, the manager.
   KIM: Hello.
   MR BROWN: So, you are interested in the job as a car mechanic. Tell me something about yourself.
5 KIM: Well, I'm sixteen years old and I'll finish school this summer. My favourite subject is maths and I am also very good at science. In my free time I play field hockey and I also like go-kart racing.
   MR BROWN: Why do you want to be a car mechanic? It's not a typical job for girls, is it?
10 KIM: Everyone keeps telling me that. But I have always been interested in cars. For years, now, I've been helping my dad repair our family car. I did my work experience at our local garage. I'm good at working with my hands and I don't mind getting them dirty.
   MR BROWN: Well, that sounds promising. Do you think you are strong enough to
15 do the job?
   KIM: Oh, I noticed when I worked in the garage that modern tools do most of the heavy work for you.
   MR BROWN: I see. Well, do you have any questions about the job?
   KIM: Hmm ... yes. What are the working hours?
20 MR BROWN: We work from 8 am till 5 pm Mondays to Fridays with an hour's break for lunch. You have three weeks' holiday a year. At the beginning you will get £ 125 a week, but your salary will be a little higher next year. When would you be able to start?
   KIM: The first of September, if that is all right with you.

25　MR BROWN: Oh yes, that would be perfect. I will need to have a closer look at your application and references. I'll let you know my decision by Monday. Is that OK?
KIM: Yes, thank you Mr Brown.
MR BROWN: Well, Kim ... thank you very much for coming along. Goodbye.
KIM: Goodbye.
30　MR BROWN: Perhaps we'll see each other again in September ...

Hinweis: *Beantworte die Fragen in Stichpunkten (Wort- oder Ziffernangabe). Achte auf die Fragewörter.*

1. this summer/in the summer
   Hinweis: *siehe Z. 5; when? (= wann?)*
2. (her) dad/father
   Hinweis: *siehe Z. 11; who? (= wer?)*
3. modern tools
   Hinweis: *siehe Z. 16 f.; what? (= was?)*
4. (£) 125 (a) week
   Hinweis: *siehe Z. 22; how much? (= wie viel?)*
5. 1(st) September/September 1(st)/the first of September
   Hinweis: *siehe Z. 24; when?*
6. Monday
   Hinweis: *siehe Z. 26; when?*

Part 4 – Aufgabe 4

1　KIM: Good morning, how can I help you?
CUSTOMER: Good morning. My car is making a strange noise. Could you have a look at it?
KIM: Yes, but not until this afternoon. Can you leave your car here?
5　CUSTOMER: Oh, no, I definitely need my car. Can't you take a look at it now?
KIM: Hmm, ... we're rather busy this morning. Er, Dave! Could you help us a moment?
DAVID: Yes? Good morning. As Kim said, we're rather busy. If you leave your car here, we can let you have a rental car. It's only £ 27.50 per day, including 200
10　miles and insurance.
CUSTOMER: Er, ... is it like my car?
DAVID: Well, in fact it's the same car, just an older model but with automatic and air conditioning.
CUSTOMER: And what about the fuel?

DAVID: We prefer you to return the car full. Otherwise we charge an extra £ 50. It's a diesel, by the way. We'll contact you as soon as we know what is wrong with your car. Could you leave your phone number with us?
CUSTOMER: Yes, of course. But ... please don't call before 2 pm.
DAVID: That's fine. Now you only need to show me your driver's license and your credit card ...

✏ **Hinweis:** *Hier musst du die fehlenden Angaben in ein Formular eintragen.*

1. 27.50
   ✏ Hinweis: Z. 9
2. air conditioning
   ✏ Hinweis: Z. 13
3. diesel
   ✏ Hinweis: Z. 15 f.
4. 50
   ✏ Hinweis: Z. 15
5. 2 pm
   ✏ Hinweis: Z. 18

B Use of English

✏ **Allgemeiner Hinweis:** *In diesem Prüfungsteil werden deine Wortschatz- und Grammatikkenntnisse getestet. Als Aufgabenform liegen dir Texte vor, in denen fehlende Wörter ergänzt oder sprachliche Fehler verbessert werden müssen. Dieser Aufgabentyp ist anspruchsvoll, da gleichzeitig Wortschatz, Grammatik und Rechtschreibung überprüft werden und die Inhalte nicht eingegrenzt sind (z. B. auf ein spezielles Grammatikthema).*

Aufgabe 1

✏ **Hinweis:** *Lies dir zunächst den Lückentext durch und versuche, den Inhalt grob zu verstehen. Anschließend gehst du die E-Mail erneut durch, diesmal Satz für Satz. Überlege dabei, welches Wort im Satzzusammenhang einen Sinn ergibt. Muss dieses Wort noch (z. B. durch Verwendung einer bestimmten Zeitform) in den Satz eingepasst werden?*
(1) „for" gibt einen Zeitraum an (hier: „für die nächsten zwei Wochen")
(2) „if/whether" = „ob"; ebenfalls möglich: „and"
(3) „than" → Steigerung/Vergleich (hier: „mehr als ...")

(4) „works/is" (Simple present); „worked/was" (Simple past) ist ebenfalls möglich, wenn ausgedrückt werden soll, dass der Gastvater früher einmal in der Firma gearbeitet hat

(5) „has ... improved" (Present perfect) → Seit („since") Martin in England ist, hat sich sein Englisch schon verbessert (etwas hat also in der Vergangenheit begonnen und wirkt sich auf die Gegenwart aus).

(6) „will ... recommend" (Will-future) → „When I'm back home" zeigt ein zukünftiges Ereignis an; im Hauptsatz muss dann das Will-future stehen.

(7) „looking forward to hearing" → feststehende Redewendung mit -ing-Form („sich freuen auf")

Hello Julia,

How are you? I (0) **am** writing to you from Birmingham. I'll be here (1) **for** the next two weeks. My company asked me (2) **if/whether/and** I was interested in working in Britain this summer. As you can imagine, I was more (3) **than** happy. I'm staying with a very nice family and the host father (4) **works/worked/is/was** in the same factory. I am the only German here so I have to talk English all the time. I think my English (5) **has** already improved quite a lot since I arrived here. I am really enjoying my stay and I love working here.

When I'm back home I (6) **will** definitely recommend such a visit to my colleagues. I am looking forward to (7) **hearing** from you soon.

Love,
Martin

Aufgabe 2

Hinweis: *Hier musst du aus den Wörtern im Kasten das jeweils passende Wort für die Lücken im Text auswählen. Es stehen dabei mehr Wörter zur Auswahl, als du brauchst. Überlege zunächst, welches Wort du in deiner Muttersprache auswählen würdest. Finde dann das richtige englische Wort und füge es ein.*

(1) abroad (= im Ausland)
(2) because of (= wegen)
(3) while (= während)
(4) could spend time (= könnten Zeit verbringen)
(5) <u>at</u> my aunt's = (<u>bei</u> meiner Tante)
(6) in <u>that</u> area (= in <u>dieser</u> Gegend)
(7) think about (= hier: halten von)

Dear Martin,

What a pleasant surprise (0) **having** you here in Britain. Did all the trainees have the chance to work (1) **abroad** or did your company choose you (2) **because** of your excellent results in your exams? You have to tell me more about it.
I would love to see you (3) **while** you are here. I could come to Birmingham next weekend so that we could (4) **spend** some time together. I could stay (5) **at** my aunt's. Have I ever mentioned that my mum's sister and her family live in (6) **that** area? My cousin Jo told me about an amusement park which is interesting and not far away. What do you think (7) **about** spending a day there? Perhaps together with Jo? If you like my idea or if you have any other suggestions, please write back soon, so we can fix a date.
Love,
Julia

Aufgabe 3

✏ **Hinweis:** *Hier sollst du in einem Brief sechs Grammatikfehler finden, die du auch verbessern musst. An den Linien in der rechten Spalte, auf die du die richtigen Wörter schreiben sollst, erkennst du leicht, in welcher Zeile sich ein Fehler befindet. Die Fehler lassen sich meist aus dem Satzzusammenhang erklären.*
In der folgenden Lösung findest du den Brief mit den unterstrichenen Fehlern. Danach folgen die richtigen Wörter (1–6) mit Hinweisen.

Dear all,

I arrived home safely after a pleasant flight, although the departure was delayed for **0.** <u>much</u> than one hour. Unfortunately, my suitcase was not on the plane, but **1.** <u>he</u> was delivered to my house by the airline later. So I was able to give the presents to my family. My grandma **2.** <u>love</u> the teapot and especially the tea.
My brother immediately put on the football shirt of the English national team and **3.** <u>doesn't</u> want to take it off again until he went to bed. My father and my sister liked **4.** <u>her</u> gifts, too.
I am so grateful that you helped me to find souvenirs for everybody. My visit went by very quickly and I've already **5.** <u>be</u> back at work **6.** <u>since</u> five days, but I have so many pleasant memories of my stay in England.
Best regards and thanks from my parents.
Love,
Martin

0. more
   Hinweis: more than = mehr als (Steigerung)
1. it
   Hinweis: suitcase → it
2. loves/loved
   Hinweis: my grandma (= she) = 3. Person Singular → love<u>s</u> (Simple present); oder: lov<u>ed</u> (Simple past)
3. didn't/did not
   Hinweis: went to bed (Simple past) → gleiche Zeit verwenden: didn't/did not
4. their
   Hinweis: father and sister = 3. Person Plural → their (Possessivpronomen)
5. been
   Hinweis: I'<u>ve</u> <u>been</u> (Present perfect)
6. for
   Hinweis: five days = Zeitraum → for

C Reading Comprehension

Allgemeiner Hinweis: In diesem Prüfungsteil stellst du dein Leseverstehen unter Beweis, indem du Aufgaben zum Grob- und Detailverständnis bearbeitest. Beim ersten Durchlesen gewinnst du einen Überblick, worum es im Text geht. Wenn du den Text ein zweites Mal liest, konzentriere dich darauf, ihn möglichst genau zu verstehen. Dann beginnst du mit dem dazugehörigen Aufgabenteil. Suche diejenigen Abschnitte oder Stellen im Text heraus, auf die sich die Aufgabe bezieht. Oft kannst du Satzteile, Angaben oder Wörter direkt aus dem Text als Antwort übernehmen und auf diese Weise z. B. Rechtschreibfehler vermeiden.

Vokabelhinweise:

Du findest nachfolgend eine Liste mit schwierigen Vokabeln aus dem Text. Zur Vorbereitung auf die Prüfung solltest du aber versuchen, möglichst viele Wörter aus dem Zusammenhang zu erschließen, sowie den Umgang mit dem Wörterbuch einzuüben. Aus Zeitgründen kannst du in der schriftlichen Prüfung nur die Wörter nachschlagen, die du unbedingt zum Verständnis benötigst.

Z. 1: entertainment: Unterhaltung
Z. 3: funfair: Jahrmarkt
Z. 5: influence: Einfluss
Z. 15: to include: enthalten, etwas aufnehmen
Z. 17: educational purpose: Bildungs-/erzieherischer Zweck
Z. 23: enclosed: hier: überdacht, sich im Innern befindend
Z. 24: Ferris wheel: Riesenrad
Z. 24: common: hier: verbreitet

Z. 27: admission fee: Eintrittspreis
Z. 30: to charge: berechnen
Z. 30 f.: to be entitled: berechtigt sein
Z. 32: beverage: Getränk
Z. 34: latest technology: modernste/ neueste Technik
Z. 37: added: hier: hinzugefügt
Z. 42: recreational activities: Freizeitaktivitäten
Z. 43: misbehavior: Fehlverhalten
Z. 44: restriction: Beschränkung
Z. 46: restraints: hier: Sicherheitsvorrichtungen (Gurte, Bügel)
Z. 47: harness: hier: Gurt
Z. 47: lap bar: Bügel über dem Schoß
Z. 47: handrail: Handlauf, Geländer
Z. 49: belongings: hier: persönliche Dinge
Z. 51: temporary: vorübergehend
Z. 53: maintained: gewartet

Aufgabe 1

Hinweis: Ordne jedem Absatz (paragraph) die inhaltlich passende Überschrift zu.

Vokabelhinweise:
development: Entwicklung; accommodation: Unterkunft

paragraph B	paragraph C	paragraph D	paragraph E	paragraph F
2	6	7	3	4

Aufgabe 2

Hinweis: Hier musst du die Fragen mit Informationen aus dem Text beantworten. Dabei sind Kurzantworten möglich. Fragewörter (z. B. who) und Schlüsselwörter (z. B. pleasure gardens – „Lustgärten", model – „Vorbild", device – „Gerät, Apparat") geben dir einen Hinweis, nach welcher Information du im Text suchen musst.

1. rich people
   Hinweis: Z. 9
2. (the) Prater (in Vienna)
   Hinweis: Z. 10 ff.
3. dark rides/ghost trains
   Hinweis: Z. 23
4. pay-one-price (scheme)
   Hinweis: Z. 30
5. (mobile) virtual reality headsets/headsets that present 3D adventures
   Hinweis: Z. 37

Aufgabe 3

✏ **Hinweis:** *Bei dieser Aufgabe sind – ähnlich wie im Wörterbuch – verschiedene Wortbedeutungen vorgegeben. Die deutsche Bedeutung hängt davon ab, welche Funktion das Wort im Satz hat (z. B. Nomen – Namenwort, Verb – Tunwort, Adjektiv – Wiewort) und in welchem Sinnzusammenhang es im Text verwendet wird. Mithilfe der Zeilenangabe findest du das gesuchte Wort im Text. Lies und übersetze nun diesen Satz(teil), indem du jeweils eine der angegebenen Möglichkeiten verwendest. So kannst du die richtige Übersetzung herausfinden.*

1. focus (line 17)
   - ☐ Mittelpunkt *(Nomen)*
   - ☐ klar sehen *(Verb)*
   - ☐ Brennpunkt *(Nomen)*
   - ☑ sich konzentrieren *(Verb)*

   ✏ **Hinweis:** *Einige Parks <u>konzentrieren sich</u> auf urzeitliche Tiere, …*

2. drop (line 21)
   - ☐ tropfen *(Verb)*
   - ☐ Tropfen *(Nomen)*
   - ☑ Fall *(Nomen)*
   - ☐ fallen lassen *(Verb)*

   ✏ **Hinweis:** *Klassische Fahrgeschäfte sind die Achterbahnen, bei denen für gewöhnlich ein <u>tiefer Fall</u> vom höchsten Punkt aus dazugehört, …*

3. mobile (line 37)
   - ☐ Handy *(Nomen)*
   - ☑ transportabel *(Adj.)*
   - ☐ Mobile *(Nomen)*
   - ☐ flexibel *(Adj.)*

   ✏ **Hinweis:** *Fahrgäste tragen <u>transportable</u> Headsets, die eine virtuelle Realität erzeugen …*

4. fit (line 46)
   - ☑ passen *(Verb)*
   - ☐ geeignet *(Adj.)*

☐ Anfall *(Nomen)*
☐ in Form *(Adj.)*
✏ Hinweis: *Achte darauf, dass die Sicherheitsvorrichtungen gut <u>passen</u>,...*

5. board (line 53)
   ☐ Brett *(Nomen)*
   ☐ Behörde *(Nomen)*
   ☑ einsteigen *(Verb)*
   ☐ verschlafen *(Verb)*

   ✏ Hinweis: <u>Steige nicht</u> *in ein Fahrgeschäft <u>ein</u>, wenn es schlecht gewartet aussieht,...*

Aufgabe 4

✏ Hinweis: *Wähle aus den Aussagen (b–j) diejenigen fünf, die dem Lesetext <u>inhaltlich</u> entsprechen. Die Aussagen sind in derselben Reihenfolge angeordnet wie die zugehörigen Informationen im Lesetext. Um die richtigen Aussagen auszuwählen, musst du die Aussagen <u>und</u> den Lesetext genau verstanden haben. Lies die entsprechenden Textteile sorgfältig durch und schlage unbekannte Vokabeln im Wörterbuch nach. Beachte, dass die Aussagen im Text oft anders formuliert sind, aber (bei der richtigen Lösung) inhaltlich übereinstimmen.*

Beispiel:
Aussage: a) Usually amusement parks are <u>very large</u>.
Text: Z. 1 f.: „Amusement park ... in a <u>large outdoor area</u>, often <u>covering many square kilometers</u>."

1. d
   ✏ Hinweis: „animals, fish and other sea life" (Z. 18 f.) = „creatures of the ocean"
2. f
   ✏ Hinweis: „transport rides" (Z. 25 f.) = „easy way to get around"
3. h
   ✏ Hinweis: „Considering the <u>speed</u> with which society and technology are changing ... <u>expect a lot of new attractions</u> ..." (Z. 39 f.) = „<u>Fast developing</u> technology ... <u>many possibilities for future park attractions</u>"
4. i
   ✏ Hinweis: „age ... restrictions" (Z. 44) = „old enough"
5. j
   ✏ Hinweis: „stay seated" (Z. 51) = „Don't get off ..."

D Text Production

✍ **Allgemeiner Hinweis:** *Lies dir beide Aufgabenstellungen erst einmal sorgfältig durch. Entscheide dich dann <u>entweder</u> für den Brief (Bewerbungsschreiben/Lebenslauf) <u>oder</u> für die Bildergeschichte. Berücksichtige die Vorgaben, die in der Aufgabenstellung enthalten sind. Achte auf einen klaren Satzbau, abwechslungsreichen Wortschatz, sowie die Rechtschreibung. Verwende das Wörterbuch, und kontrolliere immer wieder, ob dein Text sprachlich und inhaltlich schlüssig und verständlich ist. Du erhältst Punkte sowohl auf den Inhalt als auch auf die sprachliche Gestaltung. Halte dich an den vorgeschriebenen Umfang, schreibe leserlich und achte auf eine saubere äußere Form. Die folgenden Texte sind Lösungsbeispiele.*

Correspondence: Application and CV

✍ **Hinweis:** *Diese Schreibaufgabe besteht aus einem Anschreiben (Höchstpunktzahl: 16 P.) und einem tabellarischen Lebenslauf (Höchstpunktzahl: 4 P.). Das Anschreiben verfasst du als formellen Brief, in dem du die Vorgaben der Aufgabenstellung unterbringst. Wähle außerdem eine passende Anrede (Ansprechpartner: Herr Johnson), und vergiss die Grußformel sowie deinen Namen nicht. Der Lebenslauf wird in Form einer Tabelle verfasst. Bei den Gliederungspunkten gibst du stichpunktartig Auskunft über deine Person, deine Schulbildung und weitere Aspekte. Deine Angaben können auch erfunden sein, solange sie glaubhaft wirken.*

6 November 20...

Dear Mr Johnson,

I am writing to you with regard to the holiday jobs in an amusement park which I found on your agency's website. I am interested in any type of work that includes direct contact with the park's visitors, for example explaining an attraction to them or helping them to use it.
I would like to have a holiday job in England because it would help me to improve my English. This is really important to me because I want to be a travel agent after school. I already have some work experience. Our church organised a camping trip for children last year, and I helped to take care of a group of seven girls for four days. I really liked the job.
I would have time to work in the amusement park in my Easter holidays next year (24 March – 8 April). Is it possible to have accommodation in the park, and is there a canteen for the employees?
I have included my CV, and look forward to hearing from you.

Yours sincerely,
Charlotte Müller *(185 words)*

Curriculum Vitae

Personal information	Charlotte Müller, Regnitzwall 7, 90760 Fürth
	Phone: +49-911/0102030
	Age: 15
Education	Elementary school: Grundschule Herrenstraße, Fürth
	Middle school: Franken-Mittelschule, Fürth
Practical experience	Took care of 7 children during church camping trip
	Delivery of newspapers twice a week
Special knowledge	Good in English
	Computer skills
Personal interests	Nature, dogs, travel (England & France)

(54 words)

Creative Writing: Picture and Prompts

🖋 *Hinweis: Hier musst du eine Geschichte (und <u>keine</u> Bildbeschreibung!) auf Englisch verfassen. Als Impulse für deine Geschichte liegen dir ein Bild sowie Stichwörter vor. Die Stichwörter verdeutlichen die Handlung oder geben dir Anregungen, wie du deinen Text ausgestalten kannst. An welcher Stelle in deiner Geschichte du diese Vorgaben einbringen willst, entscheidest du selbst. Die Überschrift sowie der Anfang der Geschichte sind vorgegeben. Anhand des Einleitungssatzes („Last year…") erkennst du auch, dass als Zeitform hauptsächlich das Simple past zu verwenden ist. Teile deine Geschichte in Einleitung, Hauptteil und Schluss ein. Der Umfang sollte mindestens 100 Wörter betragen. Achte darauf, dass dein Text vollständig, nachvollziehbar und gut lesbar ist. Du erhältst sowohl Punkte auf den Inhalt als auch auf die sprachliche Ausgestaltung (z. B. Wortwahl, Satzbau, Rechtschreibung).*

What a shock!

Last year Barbara took her English friend Megan to the Oktoberfest. Megan was very excited because Barbara's sister had lent her a dirndl dress. She was so happy to be wearing it that she could not stop taking pictures of Barbara and herself. When Megan saw a carousel she exclaimed: "This classic old ride would go so well with my dirndl in a photo", and bought two tickets. When the two girls were spinning around, Megan yelled, "Wow, this is great! I'm going to make a video of the two of us!" Barbara shouted back, "Cool, but don't lose your phone!", but it was already too late. The phone had slipped from Megan's hand, and fell straight onto the hat of a man wearing lederhosen. The man's wife saw the phone falling down and cried out: "Oh no, watch out!"

When the merry-go-round turned again to where the man and the woman were standing, Barbara and Megan saw that the man was holding his hat and the phone in his hands. He looked up in their direction and waved. Barbara and Megan waved back. When the ride was over, the girls went to the man. "I'm so sorry," Megan apologised. The woman was angry and wanted to shout at them, but the man just smiled and gave Megan her phone. Megan invited the couple to a "Maß" of beer. Then she took a selfie of the four of them as a special souvenir.

(244 words)

Notenschlüssel

Notenstufen	1	2	3	4	5	6
Punkte	80–68	67–55	54–41	40–27	26–13	12–0

Qualifizierender Abschluss der Mittelschule Bayern 2018
Lösungen – Englisch

A Listening

Allgemeiner Hinweis: *Jeder Hörtext wird zweimal vorgespielt. Du hast in den Pausen vor und nach den Texten ausreichend Zeit, um die Aufgabenstellungen durchzulesen bzw. die Lösungen einzutragen. Rechtschreibfehler führen nicht zu Punktverlust, solange deine Lösung verständlich und inhaltlich richtig ist.*

Part 1 – Aufgabe 1

1 **Lauren:** Hi Toby. What are your plans for the weekend?
Toby: Well, I'm going rock-climbing in the Rocky Mountains on Saturday. But I'm free on Sunday.
Lauren: Great! What about going to the zoo?
5 **Toby:** The zoo, ... hmm. I don't know. I haven't been there since I was 10.
Lauren: Well, then it's certainly time for another visit! I love Calgary Zoo. I go there almost every month. I've even got a season ticket. It's only 60 Canadian dollars and you can go as often as you like for a whole year. My younger brother loves it, too. His favorite animals are the crocodiles and the dinosaurs.
10 **Toby:** Dinosaurs?
Lauren: Yeah, well, one part of the zoo is called the *Prehistoric Park*. There are models of dinosaurs, more than 20 of them. The biggest are almost 30 metres long. The *Prehistoric Park* has just reopened though. It had been closed for seven months because of repair work. Some of the models were damaged by that horrible
15 storm last October. They have also put up some new ones. It's one of the best parts of the zoo, especially when the weather is nice.
Toby: But what if it rains?
Lauren: Oh, I've already listened to the weather forecast for this weekend. It'll be windy and cool on Saturday. But on Sunday, the weather will be perfect for a
20 visit to the zoo. It'll be sunny and warm, with temperatures above 25 degrees.
Toby: Wow, sounds great. Let's go then.
Lauren: Well, when and where shall we meet?
Toby: What about 9.30?
Lauren: The zoo doesn't open until 10 on Sundays. Let's meet at 10.30 at the zoo
25 entrance.

✏ **Hinweis:** *In jedem Satz (1–8) unterscheidet sich ein Wort vom Hörtext. Streiche das falsche Wort im Satz durch und notiere das richtige Wort aus dem Hörtext. Da manche Wörter recht ähnlich klingen, solltest du genau zuhören.*

1. I haven't been there since I was **10/ten**.
    ✏ Hinweis: Z. 5
2. I've even got a **season** ticket.
    ✏ Hinweis: Z. 7
3. It's only **60/sixty** Canadian dollars and you can go as often as you like.
    ✏ Hinweis: Z. 7 f.
4. My younger brother's favorite animals are the crocodiles and the **dinosaurs**.
    ✏ Hinweis: Z. 9
5. It had been closed for seven **months** because of repair work.
    ✏ Hinweis: Z. 13 f.
6. Some of the models were damaged by that horrible **storm** last October.
    ✏ Hinweis: Z. 14 f.
7. It'll be windy and **cool** on Saturday.
    ✏ Hinweis: Z. 18 f.
8. The zoo doesn't open **until/till** 10 on Sundays.
    ✏ Hinweis: Z. 24

Part 2 – Aufgabe 2

1 **Lauren:** Hello?
Toby: Hi, it's me.
Lauren: Toby, I'm waiting for you. You're already 10 minutes late! Where are you?
Toby: I'm sorry. I'm still in the city centre. I don't know how to get to the zoo.
5 **Lauren:** What's the problem? Just take the C-train. It's line 202. You should know that.
Toby: I know that, but there are no trains between 4th Street and City Hall on line 202 because of construction work. The service is going to reopen at 11 o'clock.
Lauren: 11 o'clock! But that means it will be almost 11.30 when you arrive here.
10 Isn't there any quicker way?
Toby: Not a chance.
Lauren: OK, but what am I going to do until you get here?
Toby: Why don't you go in? You don't have to stand around and wait for me. I know you want to see the penguins and the gorillas. I'm not really interested in

them anyway, so you can go there on your own. But don't go to the grizzly bears without me. They're my favorite animals.
Lauren: All right then. Call me when you're at the entrance. I'll come and meet you there.
Toby: There's no need for that. Let's meet on the bridge across the river. It's in the middle of the zoo. That way you won't have to walk all the way back to the entrance.
Lauren: That sounds good. See you later.
Toby: See you later. Sorry again.

Hinweis: Bei dieser Aufgabe ergänzt du mithilfe des Hörtextes fehlende Informationen. Sieh dir die unvollständigen Sätze (1–5) zunächst an. Obwohl diese Sätze nicht wortwörtlich im Hörtext vorkommen, enthalten sie dennoch Schlüsselwörter (z. B. „C-train", „favorite animals"), die auch im Hörtext vorkommen, und dir signalisieren, jetzt genau zuzuhören.

Vokabelhinweis:
construction work (Z. 8): Bauarbeiten

1. Toby has to take the C-train, line **202**.
    Hinweis: Z. 5
2. At the moment, there are no trains because of **construction work**.
    Hinweis: Z. 7 f.
3. Toby will be at the zoo at about **11.30**.
    Hinweis: Z. 9
4. Toby's favorite animals are the **grizzly bears/grizzlies**.
    Hinweis: Z. 15 f.
5. They meet on the **bridge (across the river)** in the middle of the zoo.
    Hinweis: Z. 19 f.

Part 3 – Aufgabe 3

Zookeeper: Welcome everybody, my name is Dave and I'm here to tell you a little bit about Maska the grizzly bear, one of the stars of Calgary Zoo. His name is native American and means "strong". Maska is quite heavy, even for a male grizzly, which normally reaches about 380 kg; Maska weighs almost 450. When standing on his back legs, he is more than 2 metres tall. He's also faster than you might think. He can reach a speed of 60 kilometres per hour. He could easily catch Usain Bolt.

Maska has been at Calgary Zoo for 8 years now. We don't know Maska's exact age because he was born in the wilderness. He had to be captured because he was causing problems. Wild grizzlies usually stay away from humans. But Maska was often seen near villages and even in people's gardens looking for food in trashcans. He became a risk for the people living there. Some of them wanted to kill Maska. But before that happened, Maska was brought to our zoo. Our visitors think he's great, especially the children. They love it when he plays with the red ball over there, his favorite toy, although most of the time he's quite lazy. He enjoys resting in the sun.

Maska likes all kinds of food, like all grizzlies. So, on most days, we feed him a mix of apples, oranges, carrots and nuts. He also likes fish. Of course, he gets meat, too, but only once a week. The food he loves the most is hard-boiled eggs, but we only give him these on special occasions.

If you would like to watch him enjoying his meal, please come back in the afternoon ...

Hinweis: *Diese Aufgabe erfordert hohe Konzentration, da du im Hörtext mit einer Vielzahl von Informationen (z. B. Namen, Daten) konfrontiert wirst. Du sollst aber nur genau die Wörter herausfiltern, die in Maskas Steckbrief fehlen. Orientiere dich deshalb an den Schlüsselwörtern in der Tabelle, da sie deine Aufmerksamkeit beim Hören auf die entscheidenden Stellen lenken.*

Vokabelhinweis:
Usain Bolt (Z. 7): ehemaliger Sprinter, mehrfacher Olympiasieger und Weltmeister; he had to be captured (Z. 9): er musste eingefangen werden; occasion (Z. 20): Gelegenheit, Anlass

1. (almost) 450
   Hinweis: Z. 4
2. 60/sixty
   Hinweis: Z. 6
3. villages, (people's) gardens
   Hinweis: Z. 11
4. food (in trashcans)
   Hinweis: Z. 11 f.
5. resting (in the sun)/being lazy
   Hinweis: Z. 15 f.

6. carrots
   Hinweis: Z. 18
7. once a week
   Hinweis: Z. 19

B Use of English

Allgemeiner Hinweis: Du findest in diesem Prüfungsteil Aufgaben, in denen sprachliche Fehler verbessert oder Lückentexte ergänzt werden sollen. Diese Aufgabentypen sind anspruchsvoll, da gleichzeitig ein umfangreicher Wortschatz, sichere Rechtschreibung sowie gute Kenntnisse in unterschiedlichen Grammatikbereichen benötigt werden. Beachte, dass du dabei kein Wörterbuch verwenden darfst! Auch darfst du den vorgegebenen Text nicht verändern, indem du z. B. eine ganze Zeile streichst oder neue Satzteile hinzufügst.

Aufgabe 1

Hinweis: Lies den Text zur Geschichte der Eisenbahn in Kanada zunächst einmal als Ganzes durch. Vielleicht „stolperst" du dabei bereits über Wörter, die im Textzusammenhang sprachlich falsch sind. Suche danach gezielt nach den Fehlern. Die Zeilen (1–7) im Kasten rechts zeigen dir an, in welcher Textzeile sich ein Fehler befindet. Korrigiere den Fehler, indem du das das richtige Wort neben die Nummerierung auf die jeweilige Zeile schreibst. Solltest du bei dieser Aufgabe Schwierigkeiten haben, kann es dir helfen, die Grammatikbereiche im Buch (ab Seite 69) zu wiederholen.

1. more *or* less: mehr *oder* weniger; auch möglich: more and *more*: immer mehr
2. cheaper *than*: billiger *als* → Steigerung
3. *by* train: *mit* dem Zug
4. *take* the train: einen Zug *nehmen*
5. *in/during* the first half of the last century: *in/während* der 1. Hälfte des letzten Jahrhunderts
6. children *who/that* …: Kinder, *die* … → Relativpronomen; das Relativpronomen „which" wird nur für Sachen verwendet
7. *were* able to: konnten → Plural, da sich das Verb auf die Kinder bezieht

In the early years the railway played a very important role in the development **0. of** Canada. Nowadays it is more **1. or** less / **1. and** more used to transport goods. Bus tickets are cheaper **2. than** train tickets and planes are more popular if you are short of time. But when you take the time and travel **3. by** train, the experience of traveling will certainly be unforgettable. Lots of tourists **4. take** the train through the Rocky Mountains and enjoy the incredible views of the landscape. Over the years the train has served many purposes. **5.** In/During the first half of the last century there used to be a wagon equipped with a classroom, a library and accommodation for a teacher. It traveled around the country every month and children **6.** who/that lived in remote areas **7.** were able to have at least two or three days' teaching each month before the train took the wagon to the next remote location.

Aufgabe 2

✏ **Hinweis:** Lies den Text erst einmal ganz durch, um den Inhalt grob zu erfassen. So fällt es dir leichter, die richtige Form der vorgegebenen Wörter zu finden. Achte dabei auf Signalwörter (z. B. „since") oder darauf, welche Funktion das Wort im Satz hat (z. B. Adjektiv, Adverb). Solltest du bei dieser Aufgabe Schwierigkeiten haben, kann es dir helfen, in der Kurzgrammatik (ab Seite 69) nachzusehen.

1. well-known: bekannt/berühmt
2. have been: Present perfect (Signalwort „since": „seit")
3. it offers: 3. Person Singular – das „s" muss mit!
4. to get close to sb/sth: jmd/etw nahekommen
5. easily: Adverb
6. to be included: „inbegriffen sein": Passiv
7. will not/won't forget: will-future: „... die du nicht vergessen wirst" / would not/wouldn't forget: conditional I: „... die du nicht vergessen würdest"

Watching whales is very popular with (0) **tourists**. Vancouver Island in West Canada is a (1) **well**-known place for whale watching. Quite a few agencies offer such tours. And since the 1980s these tours (2) **have been** increasingly popular among tourists. You can choose between a tour on a motor or a sailing boat. Or you can even book a helicopter tour. Of course, this is really expensive but it (3) **offers** a completely different perspective. On the boat tours you get very (4) **close** to the giants of the ocean.
It is not dangerous because these animals are quite peaceful and never attack people. You could even paddle among them in a kayak. But this can be a bit risky because a whale's normal movements could (5) **easily** turn your kayak over. 'Swimming with the whales' would then be (6) **included** in the price! An experience you (7) **will not/won't/would not/wouldn't forget** for the rest of your life. Vancouver Island is indeed worth a visit.

Aufgabe 3

Hinweis: *Im vorgegebenen Text fehlt in regelmäßigen Abständen ein Wort. Lies den Text aber erst einmal ganz durch, um den Inhalt zu erfassen. Im zweiten Schritt konzentrierst du dich auf die Sätze mit den Lücken. Du kannst den Satz (in Gedanken) in deine Muttersprache übersetzen. Wenn dir klar ist, welches Wort inhaltlich in die Lücke passt, überlegst du, wie es auf Englisch heißt. Überprüfe im letzten Schritt, ob dieses Wort noch in eine bestimmte grammatikalische Form (z. B. Mehrzahl, Vergangenheit) gebracht werden muss.*

1. Neben den Kilometern wird die Distanz auch noch in Meilen angegeben.
4. <u>took</u> place: Simple past, da Ereignis bereits vergangen („in 1984")
6. <u>have to</u> compete using similar dog sleds: <u>müssen</u> mit ähnlichen Hundeschlitten gegeneinander antreten

The Yukon Quest is (0) **the** hardest dog-sled race in the world. To get from Whitehorse to Fairbanks, which is a distance of about 1,600 km or one thousand (1) **miles**, the fastest drivers need about eight days. Some sled drivers need a few days longer but every year (2) **there** are several who have to give up. Temperatures down to minus forty degrees and heavy winds (3) **make** this race a real challenge for the humans as well as for the dogs.
The first race (4) **took** place in February 1984. The name "Yukon Quest" goes back to the historical highway to the north. During the gold rush, about a hundred and fifty years (5) **ago**, the gold seekers used sleds like the ones the Inuit had. According to the race rules, participants in the Yukon Quest today (6) **have** to compete using similar dog sleds. The race is very popular, even in Europe. In 2002, it was won by a European for the first time.

C Reading Comprehension

Allgemeiner Hinweis: *In diesem Prüfungsteil stellst du dein Leseverstehen unter Beweis, indem du Aufgaben zum allgemeinen und detaillierten Verständnis bearbeitest. Beim ersten Durchlesen gewinnst du einen Überblick, worum es im Text geht. Konzentriere dich beim zweiten Lesen darauf, den Inhalt möglichst genau zu verstehen. Dann beginnst du mit dem dazugehörigen Aufgabenteil. Suche diejenigen Abschnitte oder Stellen im Text heraus, auf die sich die Aufgabe bezieht. Oft kannst du Satzteile, Angaben oder Wörter direkt aus dem Text als Antwort übernehmen, und auf diese Weise z. B. Rechtschreibfehler vermeiden.*

Vokabelhinweise:
Du findest nachfolgend eine Liste mit schwierigen Vokabeln aus dem Text. Zur Vorbereitung auf die Prüfung solltest du aber versuchen, möglichst viele Wörter aus dem Zusammenhang zu erschließen, sowie den Umgang mit dem Wörterbuch einzuüben. Aus Zeitgründen kannst du in der schriftlichen Prüfung nur die Wörter nachschlagen, die du unbedingt zum Verständnis benötigst.

Z. 3: Inuit: Selbstbezeichnung der Ureinwohner der kanadischen Arktis
Z. 6: remote: entlegen
Z. 10: to suffer from: an etwas leiden
Z. 10: principal: Schulleiter/in
Z. 11: conditions: Verhältnisse
Z. 12: majority: Mehrheit
Z. 15: temporary foster mother: Pflegemutter auf Zeit
Z. 16: promising results: erfolgsversprechende Ergebnisse
Z. 17: to benefit from sth: von etw profitieren
Z. 18: regular hours: reguläre Arbeitszeiten
Z. 20 f.: relationship: Beziehung
Z. 21: to continue: andauern, weiterbestehen
Z. 22: to deal with sth: mit etwas umgehen, sich um etwas kümmern
Z. 27: to assemble: zusammenbauen, montieren
Z. 28: to relieve: lindern
Z. 29: benefit: Vorteil
Z. 29: praise: Lob
Z. 30: self-confidence: Selbstvertrauen
Z. 36: digital access: Zugang zu digitalen Medien
Z. 37: to struggle: kämpfen
Z. 38: behavior: Verhalten
Z. 41: to transform sth: etwas umwandeln, verwandeln
Z. 42 f.: to receive: erhalten
Z. 43: award: Preis, Auszeichnung
Z. 43 f.: nomination: Vorschlag, Nominierung

Aufgabe 1

Hinweis: *In der folgenden Aufgabe sind dir unvollständige Sätze vorgegeben, die sich zwar auf den Lesetext beziehen, dort aber etwas anders formuliert sind. Lies dir zunächst die unvollständigen Sätze durch und frage dich: Wovon handelt der Satz? Welche Schlüsselwörter enthält er, die ich im Lesetext finden muss?*
Beispiel (0): Schlüsselwörter: Salluit, Quebec
Suche diese Wörter nun im Lesetext: Beispiel (0): "... <u>Salluit</u>, an Inuit village in northern <u>Quebec</u>. Salluit is a <u>small village</u> in the Canadian Arctic ..." (Z. 3 f.)
Schaue dir nun die Auswahlmöglichkeiten der Aufgabe an. Welches Wort oder welcher Satzteil deckt sich mit der Aussage im Lesetext bzw. welche Möglichkeit kann gar nicht stimmen? Im Beispiel ist die richtige Lösung „small village". Wenn du dir nicht

sicher bist, kann es helfen, Wörter im Wörterbuch nachzuschlagen, da man manchmal die Bedeutung verwechselt. Notfalls kannst du bei diesem Aufgabentyp auch in irgendeinem der Kästchen dein Häkchen setzen, vielleicht tippst du ja richtig.

1. In Salluit the climate is rough, sometimes the temperature … −25 °C.
   - [ ] is colder than
   - [ ] goes below
   - [x] even reaches
   - [ ] is less than

   ✏ Hinweis: Z. 6; „even reaches" = „erreicht sogar"

2. The prize was handed over to Maggie MacDonnell in …
   - [ ] Quebec
   - [ ] Hawaii
   - [x] Dubai
   - [ ] Salluit

   ✏ Hinweis: Z. 42 f.

3. The Global Teacher Prize has existed for … years.
   - [ ] two
   - [x] four
   - [ ] seven
   - [ ] ten

   ✏ Hinweis: Z. 44 f.

4. The prize wants to show that teachers are … for society.
   - [x] valuable
   - [ ] expensive
   - [ ] dangerous
   - [ ] responsible

   ✏ Hinweis: Z. 45 f.; „valuable" = „wertvoll" = „important role"

Aufgabe 2

Hinweis: *Im Lesetext ist jeder Absatz mit einem Buchstaben (A–F) gekennzeichnet. Deine Aufgabe ist es, die Fragen (1–5) genau dem Absatz zuzuordnen, der diese Frage beantwortet.*
1. Z. 29 f.
2. Z. 15 f.
3. Z. 43 f.
4. Z. 7 f.
5. Z. 46 f.

In which paragraph do you get the information that …

0.	… Maggie MacDonnell did not have a director at her workplace in Salluit?	B
1.	… the students feel better because of the positive feedback they get?	D
2.	… some of Maggie's students live with her for a while?	C
3.	… many teachers from all over the world wanted to become the world's best teacher?	F
4.	… the furniture at her school was in need of repair?	B
5.	… a politician from her home country honored Maggie's success?	F

Aufgabe 3

Hinweis: *Beantworte die Fragen zum Lesetext. Verwende das Wörterbuch, wenn du eine Frage nicht genau verstanden hast. Suche anschließend im Lesetext, wo du Informationen zu der Frage bekommst. Wenn du die Stelle gefunden hast, unterstreiche Schlüsselwörter oder Satzteile. Schreibe deine Lösung entweder in Stichpunkten oder als ganzen Satz auf.*

1. (only) by plane
   Hinweis: Z. 4 f.
2. books
   Hinweis: Z. 8 f.
3. on the sofa (in the living room) / in the living room
   Hinweis: Z. 12 f.

4. (a) community kitchen
   ✔ Hinweis: Z. 23; „apart from" = „außer"
5. all the village's residents
   ✔ Hinweis: Z. 28; „be allowed to" = „dürfen"
6. (the) half marathon (in Hawaii)
   ✔ Hinweis: Z. 31 f.

Aufgabe 4

✔ Hinweis: *Bei dieser Aufgabe sind – ähnlich wie im Wörterbuch – verschiedene Wortbedeutungen vorgegeben. Die deutsche Bedeutung hängt davon ab, welche Funktion das englische Wort im Satz hat (z. B. Nomen – Namenwort, Verb – Tunwort, Adjektiv – Wiewort) und in welchem Sinnzusammenhang es im Text verwendet wird. Mithilfe der Zeilenangabe findest du das gesuchte Wort im Text. Lies und übersetze nun diesen Satz(teil), indem du jeweils eine der angegebenen Möglichkeiten verwendest. So kannst du die richtige Bedeutung herausfinden.*

1. face (line 7)
   - [ ] Fassade *(Nomen)*
   - [✔] gegenüberstehen *(Verb)*
   - [ ] Gesicht *(Nomen)*
   - [ ] zeigen nach *(Verb)*

   ✔ Hinweis: "this remote settlement <u>faces</u> some serious social problems" = „diese entlegene Siedlung <u>steht</u> einigen ernsthaften sozialen Problemen <u>gegenüber</u>"

2. end (line 20)
   - [✔] aufhören *(Verb)*
   - [ ] beenden *(Verb)*
   - [ ] Ende *(Nomen)*
   - [ ] Ziel *(Nomen)*

   ✔ Hinweis: "as a teacher in a small Arctic village your day never <u>ends</u>" = „für einen Lehrer in einem kleinen arktischen Dorf <u>hört</u> der Tag nie <u>auf</u>/<u>endet</u> der Tag nie"

3. service (line 25)
   - [ ] Bedienung *(Nomen)*
   - [x] Dienstleistung *(Nomen)*
   - [ ] instand halten *(Verb)*
   - [ ] Wartung *(Nomen)*

   ✏ **Hinweis:** *"and also provides a useful <u>service</u> to the community"* = „und stellt der Gemeinde auch eine nützliche <u>Dienstleistung</u> zur Verfügung"

4. spend (line 31)
   - [ ] Ausgabe *(Nomen)*
   - [ ] ausgeben *(Verb)*
   - [ ] verbrauchen *(Verb)*
   - [x] verbringen *(Verb)*

   ✏ **Hinweis:** *"Ms. MacDonnell <u>spends</u> a lot of time as a coach for the Salluit Running Club"* = „Ms. MacDonnell <u>verbringt</u> viel Zeit als Trainerin des Laufvereins von Salluit"

5. level (line 34)
   - [ ] eben *(Adjektiv)*
   - [x] Ebene *(Nomen)*
   - [ ] gleichmachen *(Verb)*
   - [ ] Pegel *(Nomen)*

   ✏ **Hinweis:** *"connect on a person-to-person <u>level</u>"* = „sich auf einer persönlichen <u>Ebene</u> verbinden"

D Text Production

✏ **Allgemeiner Hinweis:** Lies dir beide Aufgabenstellungen erst einmal gut durch. Entscheide dich dann <u>entweder</u> für den Brief <u>oder</u> für die Bildergeschichte. Berücksichtige die Vorgaben, die in der Aufgabenstellung enthalten sind. Achte auf einen klaren Satzbau, abwechslungsreichen Wortschatz sowie die Rechtschreibung. Verwende das Wörterbuch, und kontrolliere immer wieder, ob dein Text sprachlich und inhaltlich schlüssig und verständlich ist. Du erhältst sowohl für den Inhalt als auch auf die sprachliche Gestaltung Punkte. Halte dich an den vorgeschriebenen Umfang, schreibe leserlich und achte auf eine saubere äußere Form. Die folgenden Texte sind Lösungsbeispiele.

Correspondence: Letter

✎ **Hinweis:** *Bei dieser Schreibaufgabe liegt ein Brief von Sam vor, dem du ebenfalls in Form eines Briefes antworten sollst. In deinem Antwortbrief gehst du auf die Dinge ein, die dein Brieffreund von dir wissen will. Überlege dir ebenfalls, was du über Sam erfahren willst.*
Im ersten Schritt gehst du Sams Brief in Ruhe durch und markierst, was er von dir wissen will. Sammle Ideen, was du darauf antworten könntest. Mache dir dann Gedanken, welche Fragen du an Sam hast.
Beginne nun mit dem Schreiben, indem du das Datum notierst und die Anrede verfasst. Was den Aufbau betrifft, kannst du dich an Sams Brief orientieren.
Wähle für den Hauptteil aus deiner „Ideensammlung" die Punkte aus, zu denen dir inhaltlich und sprachlich viel einfällt. Schreibe in ganzen, vollständigen Sätzen. Kontrolliere deinen Brief am Ende noch einmal: Ist er interessant zu lesen, vollständig und verständlich? Hast du dich verabschiedet?

30 June 2018

Hi Sam,

Thanks for your letter! My name is Tobias, I'm 16 years old and I live in Regensburg. This is a very old city in the east of Bavaria. The Danube flows through it, which is the second longest river in Europe.

I have a lot of hobbies. Now in summer I like to be outside with my friends and do various kinds of activities. What I like best is going to the high ropes course. We have such courses in Regensburg but also in other places in Bavaria. Have you ever tried it? You climb up trees and move from one tree to the next on planks, pendant bridges or ropes. It is very exciting but also safe because your body is always fixed with a rope. I also like swimming and cycling along the Danube.

You also asked about my plans for the future. I'll graduate from school soon, but I haven't found an apprenticeship place yet. I want to become a carpenter.

I'd like to have a penfriend in Canada because I'm interested in this beautiful country, and I'd like to improve my English by writing to you.

What is it like to live in Kelowna? Is it close to the sea? Do you also learn a foreign language at school?

I'm looking forward to your reply!

Take care,

Tobias

(224 words)

Creative Writing: Picture Story

✏ **Hinweis:** *Bei dieser Schreibaufgabe sollst du die Informationen und Ideen, die du den sechs Bildern entnehmen kannst, in Form einer zusammenhängenden Geschichte erzählen. Betrachte zunächst jedes einzelne Bild genau und notiere dir einige Schlüsselwörter dazu. Auch Einzelheiten können für die Handlung wichtig sein. Überlege dann, welche Bilder du der Einleitung, dem Hauptteil und dem Schluss zuordnen würdest. Ändere dabei aber keinesfalls die vorgegebene Reihenfolge der Bilder!*
Der Hauptteil beginnt normalerweise bei dem Bild, ab dem die Geschichte spannend wird, weil etwas Unerwartetes passiert. Diesen Teil solltest du ausführlich erzählen. Überlege dir schließlich, wie deine Geschichte endet.
Achte darauf, die Überschrift und den Anfangssatz aus der Aufgabe zu übernehmen. Lass die Personen in der Geschichte miteinander sprechen („wörtliche Rede") um deine Erzählung lebendig zu machen. Die folgende Geschichte ist eine Beispiellösung. So könnte z. B. die Keksdose auch eine Packung Chips sein.

A hungry squirrel

One day in winter Katie and her brother Jim were sitting in the igloo which they had built next to their house. Inside the igloo it was not very cold, so they sat on their jackets while eating cookies out of a tin. When their mom called them inside for dinner, they forgot to take the tin and their jackets with them.

Early the next morning they had to get ready for school. Their mom pointed at the empty coat-hooks and asked "Where are your jackets, kids?" "I think we have left them in the igloo", Katie remembered and went out into the garden with Jim and mom. The jackets were still inside the igloo. But what was that? A little squirrel was sitting on one of the jackets, eating cookies from the tin and leaving crumbs all over. The jackets had become quite messy. At first Katie was upset and wanted to chase away the squirrel, but then she felt sorry for the hungry animal and so the family allowed it to finish its meal.

However, Katie and Jim had no idea how to get to school without their warm jackets!

(195 words)

Notenschlüssel

Notenstufen	1	2	3	4	5	6
Punkte	80–68	67–55	54–41	40–27	26–13	12–0

> Qualifizierender Abschluss der Mittelschule Bayern 2019
> Lösungen – Englisch

A Listening

🖉 **Allgemeiner Hinweis:** *Jeder Hörtext wird zweimal vorgespielt. Du hast in den Pausen vor und nach den Texten ausreichend Zeit, um die Aufgabenstellungen durchzulesen bzw. die Lösungen einzutragen. Rechtschreibfehler führen nicht zu Punktverlust, solange deine Lösung verständlich und inhaltlich richtig ist. Bei diesem Teil darfst du <u>kein</u> Wörterbuch verwenden.*

Part 1 – Aufgabe 1

1 **Receptionist:** Portobello Hotel. Can I help you?
Marcus: Hello. Yes, I'd like to know if you have any rooms available at the end of August.
Receptionist: Let me have a look. End of August. OK, when were you thinking of
5 coming exactly?
Marcus: Um ... August 28.
Receptionist: OK. And for how many nights?
Marcus: Two.
Receptionist: Right. Is that a single or a double?
10 **Marcus:** Double, please.
Receptionist: Yes, that looks fine.
Marcus: Great. I see on the internet you charge £ 110 a night for a double. Is that right?
Receptionist: In winter, yes. But in summer they're £ 130, I'm afraid.
15 **Marcus:** Mmm. OK. And does that include breakfast?
Receptionist: Yes, of course.
Marcus: It says here that you're very close to the Underground.
Receptionist: Yes, five minutes on foot from the tube station Holland Park.
Marcus: Is that the Central Line?
20 **Receptionist:** Yes, so it's six stops to Oxford Circus.
Marcus: OK. Great.
Receptionist: So, shall we book that for you?
Marcus: Yes, please.
Receptionist: Leaving on August 30?
25 **Marcus:** That's right.
Receptionist: OK. Could I take your name, please?

✏ **Hinweis:** *Hier findest du unvollständige Aussagen, die du durch die Informationen aus dem Hörtext ergänzen sollst. Lies die Sätze zunächst genau durch und markiere Schlüsselwörter in den Aussagen (z. B. 1. come/August, 3. double room/in summer). Achte während des Hörens auf diese Schlüsselwörter und ergänze die Lücken im Satz mit der jeweils passenden Information aus dem Hörtext.*

Vokabelhinweis:
on foot (Z. 18) = zu Fuß

1. Laura and Marcus want to come to London on August **(the) 28(th)**.
   ✏ Hinweis: Z. 6
2. They want to stay at the Portobello Hotel for two **nights**.
   ✏ Hinweis: Z. 8
3. A double room costs £ **130** in summer.
   ✏ Hinweis: Z. 14
4. The hotel is five minutes **on foot** from the tube station Holland Park.
   ✏ Hinweis: Z. 18
5. From Holland Park it's six **stops** to Oxford Circus.
   ✏ Hinweis: Z. 18ff.
6. Laura and Marcus are leaving on August **(the) 30(th)**.
   ✏ Hinweis: Z. 24 f.

Part 2 – Aufgabe 2

1 **Woman:** Hello there. How can I help?
   Laura: Er … yeah … we've heard about something called a London Pass. Could you tell us what it is exactly?
   Woman: Well, it's like a smart card. It gets you into tourist attractions in London
5 without having to pay in cash every time.
   Laura: OK. So places like the Tower of London?
   Woman: Yes, exactly. And the other thing is that you don't have to queue to get in. You just walk to the front and go through.
   Laura: Oh, that's good. How much does it cost?
10 **Woman:** £ 43 a day.
   Marcus: Is a day 24 hours from when I buy the pass or is it … is it …?
   Woman: No, it's a calendar day. So if you don't pick up your card until late in the afternoon you've lost quite a lot of money.
   Laura: Mmm. OK. And can we get one here, right now?
15 **Woman:** Yes, you can. But it's 1 o'clock so …

Marcus: ... and when do you open in the morning?
Woman: 10 am.
Marcus: So we could order it now and pick it up tomorrow at 10?
Woman: Yes, of course.
20 Laura (to Marcus): Let's do that, shall we?
Woman: So that's two, is it?
Marcus: Yes, please.

Hinweis: In der Aufgabe sind Sätze vorgegeben, die sich vom jeweiligen Satz im Hörtext durch genau ein Wort unterscheiden. Konzentriere dich auf diese Sätze mit dem Ziel, während des Zuhörens die entsprechende Textstelle zu erkennen. Streiche das Wort, das sich vom Hörtext unterscheidet, sobald du es erkennst.

Vokabelhinweis:
to queue (Z. 7) = sich in der Warteschlange anstellen

1. It gets you into ~~terrific~~ attractions in London.
   Hinweis: Z. 4
2. And the ~~best~~ thing is that you don't have to queue to get in.
   Hinweis: Z. 7
3. So if you don't pick up your card until late in the ~~evening~~ ...
   Hinweis: Z. 12f.
4. And can ~~you~~ get one here?
   Hinweis: Z. 14
5. So we could order it now and pick it up tomorrow at ~~11~~?
   Hinweis: Z. 18

Part 3 – Aufgabe 3

1 Receptionist: Hello.
Marcus: Hello. Could you help me with some directions, please?
Receptionist: Yes, sure. Where do you want to go?
Marcus: The Tower of London.
5 Receptionist: On the tube?
Marcus: Yeah. And it says here that the nearest station is Tower Hill.
Receptionist: OK.
Marcus: So shall we go this way round ... on the Circle Line or ...?

Receptionist: You can do. But it takes quite a long time. And you have to change once.
Marcus: OK. What would you suggest?
Receptionist: Well, if you take the Central Line and go to Bank, that's the station here, it's much quicker and you don't have to change.
Marcus: Oh, I see. That's ... one, two, three ... eleven stations.
Receptionist: Yeah. The only problem is ...
Marcus: Yeah?
Receptionist: You have to walk a bit from Bank station to the Tower.
Marcus: OK. How far?
Receptionist: Um ... about fifteen minutes I'd say. But all in all it's probably quicker than the other route, you know, going round here on the Circle Line.
Marcus: And we get some exercise, too.
Receptionist: Yeah, that as well!

Hinweis: Um die Fragen beantworten zu können, musst du sie inhaltlich verstehen („which?" = „welche?", „how long?" = „wie lange?"). Nur so weißt du, auf welche Informationen du während des Hörens achten musst. Ein weiterer Anhaltspunkt sind Schlüsselwörter aus den Fragen („line" = „U-Bahn-Linie"; walk, Bank station, Tower), da diese auch im Hörtext vorkommen und deine Aufmerksamkeit auf die jeweils richtige Textstelle lenken.

Vokabelhinweise:
directions (Z. 2) = Wegbeschreibung
on the tube (Z. 5) = mit der U-Bahn
to change (Z. 9) = umsteigen
to suggest (Z. 11) = vorschlagen

1. Central Line
   Hinweis: Z. 11 f.
2. 15 minutes
   Hinweis: Z. 17 ff.

Part 4 – Aufgabe 4

1 **Guest:** Your last day, then?
   Marcus: Yes, it is. Have you just arrived?
   Guest: Yes, last night.
   Laura: And how long are you staying?
5 **Guest:** For a week. We come every year actually. And always in August.
   Marcus: You must know London very well.
   Guest: Yes, we do. We love it here.
   Laura: And do you go sightseeing when you're here?
   Guest: Well, we know all the main attractions very well; the London Eye, the
10   Crown Jewels and so on.
   Laura: Yeah.
   Guest: Now we like going to museums. There're so many of them in London. And most of them are free.
   Marcus: You mean the British Museum?
15 **Guest:** Well, that's the most famous one. But there are others. The Science Museum is great. And the Natural History Museum, too.
   Laura: So what have you got planned for today?
   Guest: Well, this morning we want to go to the Museum of London.
   Marcus: The Museum of London? Where's that?
20 **Guest:** Not far from St Paul's Cathedral. So, easy to get to from here.
   Marcus: Well, have a good day.
   Guest: Thanks. You have a good flight, too.
   Marcus & Laura: Thanks.

Hinweis: Entscheide bei dieser Aufgabe, welche Aussagen zum Hörtext richtig oder falsch sind. Beachte, dass die Aussagen in der Aufgabe nur sinngemäß formuliert sind, d. h. mit anderen Worten als im Hörtext (z. B. sights ↔ attractions, travel home by plane ↔ flight).

Vokabelhinweis:
museums ... are free (Z. 12 f.) = hier: freier Eintritt

	T	F
1. The guest arrived at the hotel this morning. *Hinweis: Z. 2 f.*		✓
2. The guest wants to stay in London for a week. *Hinweis: Z. 4 f.*	✓	

		T	F
3.	The guest knows the main sights in London well. *Hinweis: Z. 9*	✓	☐
4.	All museums in London are free. *Hinweis: Z. 12 f.*	☐	✓
5.	The British Museum is the most famous museum in London. *Hinweis: Z. 14 f.*	✓	☐
6.	This morning the guest wants to go to St Paul's Cathedral. *Hinweis: Z. 18*	☐	✓
7.	Laura and Marcus travel home by plane. *Hinweis: Z. 22*	✓	☐

B Use of English

Allgemeiner Hinweis: Anders als in den Vorjahren ist der Prüfungsteil diesmal so gegliedert, dass pro Aufgabe immer nur ein Teilgebiet geprüft wird: Wortschatz (Aufgaben 1, 2), ein Grammatikbereich (Aufgaben 3, 4) sowie ein Dialog (Aufgabe 5). Beachte, dass du kein Wörterbuch verwenden darfst. Rechtschreibfehler führen zu Punktabzug. Ausnahmen gelten bei anerkannter Rechtschreibstörung.

Aufgabe 1

Hinweis: In dieser Aufgabe geht es um Präpositionen und Konjunktionen. Welches Wort du verwenden musst, ergibt sich aus dem Satzzusammenhang. Die Präpositionen sind oft Teil einer festen Verbindung.
1. born <u>on</u> ... = geboren <u>am</u> ... (Präposition)
2. good <u>at</u> ... = gut <u>in</u> ...(Präposition)
3. when = als / although = obwohl (Konjunktionen)
4. get a job <u>as</u> a ... = eine Arbeit <u>als</u> ... bekommen (Präposition)

The US rock singer Gwen Stefani was born (0) **in** Orange County, California (1) **on** October 3rd, 1969. She has got three brothers and sisters and they are all good (2) **at** music. Eric, one of Gwen's brothers, started the band called *No Doubt*. Gwen became the band's lead singer (3) **when/although** she was only 18. In 1995 Eric left the band because he got a job (4) **as** a cartoon artist.

Aufgabe 2

✏ **Hinweis:** *Bei dieser Wortschatzaufgabe wird das gesuchte Wort mit einer Definition umschrieben. Der Anfangsbuchstabe und die Anzahl der Buchstaben sind als Hilfe vorgegeben. Notiere die einzelnen Buchstaben des gesuchten Wortes auf den vorgegebenen Strichen.*
2. return ticket = Hin- und Rückfahrkarte

1. station
2. **return** ticket
3. late
4. passenger

Aufgabe 3

✏ **Hinweis:** *Hier sind überwiegend zusammengesetzte Wörter mit „some" und „any" vorgegeben. Der Unterschied liegt in der grammatikalischen Verwendung. Vereinfacht gilt folgende Regel: „Some" verwendest du in Aussagen und bejahten Sätzen, „any" in Fragen und verneinten Sätzen.*
0. everyone = jede(r), hier auch: alle
1. anywhere = nirgendwo (wegen Verneinung „could<u>n't</u> see Tim anywhere")
2. everywhere = überall
3. something = etwas
4. anything = nichts (wegen Verneinung „had<u>n't</u> had anything")

Susan and Tim went surfing with some friends and (0) **everyone** had a lot of fun. Suddenly Susan couldn't see Tim (1) **anywhere**. She looked for him (2) **everywhere**. Then she saw him at a hamburger stall. He was buying (3) **something** to eat because he hadn't had (4) **anything** for breakfast.

Aufgabe 4

✏ **Hinweis:** *Dies ist eine Aufgabe zum Grammatikbereich „tenses" – Zeiten. In Klammern ist die Grundform eines englischen Verbs (Tunworts) vorgegeben. Lies dir zunächst die zusammengehörenden Sätze jedes Absatzes genau durch, da zeitlich zum Teil Bezug auf den vorherigen bzw. nachfolgenden Satz genommen wird. Unterstreiche außerdem Signalwörter, die darauf hinweisen, welche englische Zeitform verwendet werden muss. Beachte auch Besonderheiten, z. B. im „simple present" (he, she, it → Verb +„s").*
1. every year (Signalwort), the club offer<u>s</u> („simple present")

2. ever (Signalwort für „present perfect")
3. last year (Signalwort für „simple past")
4. this time (hier: Signalwort für „simple present")

Brenda (0) **is** a member of a youth club. Every year the club (1) **offers** summer activities.
At the moment Brenda and her friends are sitting on the train to Brighton. A friendly lady starts talking to them. She asks Brenda, "(2) **Have** you ever **been** to Brighton?"
Brenda answers, "Unfortunately not. It's my first time. Last year I was on holiday near Brighton but I (3) **did not/didn't go** to Brighton itself. So this time I (4) **want** to do some sightseeing."

Aufgabe 5

Hinweis: In dem Dialog sind die Fragen, die Chris stellt, bereits in der richtigen Reihenfolge angegeben. Du musst nur noch die passenden Antworten (A–H) auf Alex' Seite finden und in die Tabelle eintragen. Achte darauf, dass der Dialog logisch ist und einen Sinn ergibt.

Vokabelhinweis:
to spend money = Geld ausgeben

0	1	2	3	4	5
C	D	B	F	E	H

C Reading Comprehension

Allgemeiner Hinweis: In diesem Prüfungsteil stellst du dein Leseverstehen unter Beweis, indem du Aufgaben zum allgemeinen und detaillierten Verständnis bearbeitest. Beim ersten Durchlesen gewinnst du einen Überblick, worum es im Text geht. Konzentriere dich beim zweiten Lesen darauf, den Inhalt möglichst genau zu verstehen. Dann beginnst du mit dem dazugehörigen Aufgabenteil. Suche diejenigen Abschnitte oder Stellen im Text heraus, auf die sich die jeweilige Aufgabe bezieht. Vieles kannst du direkt aus dem Text als Antwort übernehmen, und auf diese Weise z. B. Rechtschreibfehler vermeiden.

Vokabelhinweise:
Du findest nachfolgend eine Liste mit schwierigen Vokabeln aus dem Text. Zur Vorbereitung auf die Prüfung solltest du aber versuchen, möglichst viele Wörter aus dem Zusammenhang zu erschließen, sowie den Umgang mit dem Wörterbuch einzuüben. Aus Zeitgründen kannst du in der schriftlichen Prüfung nur die Wörter nachschlagen, die du unbedingt zum Verständnis benötigst.

Z. 1: capsule = Kapsel, hier: Gondel
Z. 9: breathtaking = atemberaubend
Z. 11: to be scared = Angst haben
Z. 18: to board = einsteigen
Z. 20: observation wheel = Riesenrad
Z. 29: to take a flight: hier = eine Fahrt machen
Z. 30: occasion = Anlass
Z. 30: to hire = mieten
Z. 33: location = Lage
Z. 33 f.: to use for demonstrations = hier: auf sich oder ein Anliegen aufmerksam machen
Z. 38: vision = Sicht, hier: Vision (= Vorstellung)
Z. 39: aim = Ziel

Aufgabe 1

Hinweis: Der Lesetext ist in Absätze unterteilt – die genaue Unterteilung kannst du den Zeilenangaben in der Tabelle entnehmen. Jedem Absatz soll nun eine Überschrift (A–G) zugeordnet werden. Lies dir jeweils einen Absatz des Lesetextes durch und vergleiche ihn mit der Auswahl an Überschriften. Falls du nicht sofort die passende Überschrift erkennst, kannst du zuerst die Überschriften der anderen Absätze zuordnen.

Vokabelhinweise:
A: difficulties = Schwierigkeiten, to construct: bauen
E: attraction = Attraktion, Sehenswürdigkeit
F: offer = Angebot
G: exciting: aufregend, experience = Erfahrung

lines 1–15	lines 16–19	lines 20–25	lines 26–32	lines 33–36	lines 37–40
C	G	A	F	B	E

Aufgabe 2

Hinweis: *Entscheide auf Grundlage des Lesetextes, ob die Aussagen 1–4 richtig oder falsch sind oder es im Lesetext gar keinen Beleg für sie gibt. Nimm dir Zeit, die vorgegebenen Sätze zu verstehen, da sie grammatikalisch manchmal nicht ganz einfach sind.*

	T	F	N
1. The London Eye moves very fast.		✓	
2. Building the London Eye was finished before the year 2000.	✓		
3. A man was arrested after his protest in 2004.			✓
4. The London Eye is still the highest observation wheel in the world.		✓	

1. **Hinweis:** Z. 4 f. („slow climb")
2. **Hinweis:** Das „London Eye" war 1999 fertig. (Z. 24 f.)
3. **Hinweis:** was arrested = wurde verhaftet
4. **Hinweis:** still = immer noch; es gibt inzwischen ein höheres Riesenrad (Z. 37 f.)

Aufgabe 3

Hinweis: *Beantworte die Fragen mithilfe des Textes in Stichpunkten. Durchsuche den Lesetext nach der jeweiligen Antwort. Es kann hilfreich sein, die entscheidende Textstelle farblich zu markieren.*

1. half an hour / 30 minutes
    Hinweis: Z. 18
2. seven / 7 years
    Hinweis: Z. 21
3. March 2000
    Hinweis: Z. 26
4. 15,000 / 15 000
    Hinweis: Z. 29
5. birthday(s) / Christmas / wedding(s)
    Hinweis: *Von den drei möglichen Beispielen müssen zwei genannt werden. Pro Beispiel gibt es 1 Punkt, also insgesamt 2 Punkte.*
    what kind of event = welche Art von Veranstaltung; Z. 29 ff.

Aufgabe 4

🖋 **Hinweis:** *Hier wird nach Informationen aus dem Text gefragt. Stelle sicher, dass du die Fragen vollständig verstehst, indem du z. B. unbekannten Wortschatz im Wörterbuch nachschlägst. Die Reihenfolge der Fragen folgt dem Textaufbau, d. h., die Antwort auf Frage 1 steht im oberen Teil des Lesetextes, usw. Sobald du den Satz im Text gefunden hast, der die Antwort auf die zugehörige Frage beinhaltet, solltest du diesen richtig und <u>in voller Länge</u> abschreiben.*

1. If the weather is clear, you'll be able to see Windsor Castle, 38 km away.
   🖋 **Hinweis:** *Z. 14 f.*
2. From here cars, buses and taxis look like children's toys.
   🖋 **Hinweis:** *Z. 16 f.; vehicles = Fahrzeuge*
3. Over 1,700 people from five countries worked on it.
   🖋 **Hinweis:** *Z. 21 f.; people = Menschen, Leute*
4. But three and a half million people came.
   🖋 **Hinweis:** *Z. 28: Es wird nach der tatsächlichen Anzahl von Besuchern („actually visited") gefragt und nicht nach der erhofften Besucherzahl. Im Text wird auch die Angabe „Jahr" (year) statt „12 Monate" (12 months) verwendet.*
5. And for around £ 2,000 you can celebrate your wedding in a private capsule decorated with flowers.
   🖋 **Hinweis:** *Z. 31 f.*

D Text Production

🖋 **Allgemeiner Hinweis:** *Lies dir beide Aufgabenstellungen erst einmal gut durch. Entscheide dich dann <u>entweder</u> für die E-Mail <u>oder</u> für die Bildergeschichte. Berücksichtige die Vorgaben, die in der Aufgabenstellung enthalten sind. Achte auf einen klaren Satzbau, abwechslungsreichen Wortschatz sowie die Rechtschreibung. Verwende das Wörterbuch, und kontrolliere immer wieder, ob dein Text sprachlich richtig und inhaltlich schlüssig und verständlich ist. Du erhältst sowohl für den Inhalt als auch auf die sprachliche Gestaltung Punkte. Halte dich an den vorgeschriebenen Umfang, schreibe leserlich und achte auf eine saubere äußere Form. Die folgenden Texte sind Lösungsbeispiele.*

Correspondence: Email

🖊 **Hinweis:** *Halte dich den Inhalt betreffend an die verbindlichen Angaben der Aufgabe, die du durch eigene Ideen ergänzt. Eine genaue Anleitung, wie du beim Schreiben der E-Mail vorgehst, findest du im Kompetenzbereich „Text Production" im Trainingsteil des Aufgabenbandes.*

Lies die Aufgabenstellung genau durch: Der Adressat ist ein Hotel in London, dem du wegen einer vergessenen Reisetasche schreibst. Du wählst also einen formellen, höflichen Stil. Verwende eine geeignete Anrede und Schlussformel und nach Möglichkeit Langformen (z. B. „I am").

In der Aufgabe sind die Inhalte, die du erwähnen musst, bereits auf Deutsch aufgelistet. Gehe sie der Reihe nach durch. Du musst sie jedoch noch teilweise ausschmücken, indem du z. B. eine Zimmernummer erfindest oder angibst, wo die Tasche vermutlich vergessen wurde. Schlage unbekannten Wortschatz im Wörterbuch nach.

Beginne nun mit dem Schreiben. Solange du über euren zurückliegenden Aufenthalt berichtest, solltest du die „simple past"-Vergangenheit verwenden. Bei der Beschreibung der Tasche und bei der Bitte um Nachsendung ist die „simple present"-Gegenwart angemessen.

Kontrolliere zum Schluss deinen Text. Beträgt der Umfang ca. 100 Wörter? Hast du alle Angaben berücksichtigt? Hast du leserlich und verständlich geschrieben? Hast du an Anrede und Verabschiedung gedacht?

Dear Madam or Sir,

My parents and I were guests in your hotel and we enjoyed our stay with you very much. I am writing because we left behind one of our bags at your hotel when we checked out yesterday. We believe that we left the bag in room number 304 on the third floor. It could be in the wardrobe. It is a dark blue sports bag with a large white tiger on one side. There are some hiking socks and a travel guide about Wales in it. Could you please look for our bag and send it to our address (see the bottom of this email)? We would pay for the shipping costs, of course.

Please reply soon. Thank you very much in advance.

Kind regards,

Tim Baumann
Hauptstr. 62
97070 Würzburg
Germany

(136 words)

Creative Writing: Picture and prompts

✏ **Hinweis:** *Als Schreibanlass werden dir eine Zeichnung („picture") und Angaben in Form von Stichpunkten („prompts") vorgelegt. Verwende diese für eine schlüssige Geschichte. Wie du dabei genau vorgehst, kannst du im Kompetenzbereich „Text Production" im Trainingsteil des Aufgabenbandes nachlesen.*

Betrachte zuerst das Bild: Zwei Jungen entdecken in einem Geschäft einen gut gefüllten Geldbeutel, der offen auf dem Boden liegt. Überlege nun, wie Bild und Stichwörter zusammenhängen. Wie könnte es zu dieser Situation gekommen sein und wie könnte die Geschichte weitergehen? Notiere nun deine Ideen und wähle die besten aus.

Wichtig ist die Angabe „gemeinsame Entscheidung", da sie den <u>Höhepunkt der Geschichte</u> *darstellt. Sie sollte sich aus den Gedanken und Gesprächen der beiden Jungen ergeben: Entweder sind sich die beiden von Anfang an einig, wie sie mit dem Fund umgehen wollen (behalten oder zurückgeben), oder eben nicht. Auch der Stichpunkt „Vorgang an der Kasse" lässt verschiedene Möglichkeiten offen. Der Kunde an der Kasse könnte seinen Geldbeutel suchen. Die Teenager beschließen, ihren Einkauf mit dem Geld aus dem Fund zu bezahlen oder sie sind ehrliche Finder und geben den Geldbeutel an der Kasse ab.*

Schreibe nun die Geschichte im vorgeschriebenen Umfang und gliedere sie in Einleitung, Hauptteil und Schluss. Überschrift und Einleitung sind bereits vorgegeben. Daraus sind sowohl die Namen der Hauptfiguren (Paul und Jake) als auch die zu verwendende Zeitform („simple past") ersichtlich. Nutze bei Bedarf ein Wörterbuch. Verwende bei Gedanken und Gesprächen die wörtliche Rede (z. B. Paul said: "...").

Überprüfe zum Schluss, ob deine Geschichte den geforderten Umfang (ca. 100 Wörter) hat und aus Einleitung, Hauptteil (mit Spannungsbogen) und Schluss besteht. Sind alle notwendigen Informationen enthalten? Enthält sie wörtliche Rede? Ist deine Geschichte gut lesbar und nachvollziehbar, auch wenn man das Bild und die Angaben nicht kennt?

Der folgende Text ist eine Beispiellösung. Er ist bewusst umfangreicher gehalten, als in der Aufgabe gefordert. Dies soll dir Ideen für deine eigene Geschichte geben und es dir ermöglichen, deinen Wortschatz zu erweitern.

Lost and found

Last Saturday afternoon Paul and Jake were in a games shop. Suddenly Jake saw a wallet.
"Look at this, Paul, there's a wallet on the floor!" Jake exclaimed and thought he should pick it up before anybody else did.
"Hush, be quiet" Paul said.
Jake picked up the wallet. There were some credit cards and some 50 pound notes in it.

Paul said: "You're not thinking of keeping it?"
"Why not?" Jake answered.
"Someone is missing it!" Paul said.
"Ah, come on! I just found this great new video game and I don't have the money to buy it. With the cash in that wallet I could …"
Paul said: "Forget about it! We have to report that we found it."
"OK, OK, you're right." Jake gave in.
At the check-out a customer was very upset. He wanted to pay but couldn't find his wallet. He was so happy when the boys arrived at the check-out with it. As a reward the man asked them to choose one of the video games. Jake knew exactly which one to take!

(165 words)

Notenschlüssel

Notenstufen	1	2	3	4	5	6
Punkte	80–68	67–55	54–41	40–27	26–13	12–0

Qualifizierender Abschluss der Mittelschule Bayern 2020
Lösungen – Englisch

Das Corona-Virus hat im vergangenen Schuljahr auch die Prüfungsabläufe durcheinandergebracht und manches verzögert. Daher sind die Lösungen zur Prüfung 2020 in diesem Jahr nicht im Buch abgedruckt, sondern erscheinen in digitaler Form.

Sobald die Original-Prüfungsaufgaben 2020 zur Veröffentlichung freigegeben sind, können die Lösungen zur Prüfung 2020 als PDF auf der Plattform **MyStark** heruntergeladen werden. Deinen persönlichen Zugangscode findest du auf der Umschlaginnenseite.

Prüfung 2020

www.stark-verlag.de/mystark

ONLINE LERNEN
mit **STARK** und StudySmarter

STARK LERNINHALTE GIBT ES AUCH ONLINE!

Deine Vorteile:
- ✔ Auch einzelne Lerneinheiten – sofort abrufbar
- ✔ Gratis Lerneinheiten zum Testen

WAS IST STUDYSMARTER?

StudySmarter ist eine intelligente **Lern-App** und **Lernplattform**, auf der du ...
- ✔ deine Mitschriften aus dem Unterricht hochladen,
- ✔ deine Lerninhalte teilen und mit der Community diskutieren,
- ✔ Zusammenfassungen, Karteikarten und Mind-Maps erstellen,
- ✔ dein Wissen täglich erweitern und abfragen,
- ✔ individuelle Lernpläne anlegen kannst.

Google Play

Apple App Store

StudySmarter – die Lern-App kostenlos bei Google Play oder im Apple App Store herunterladen. Gleich anmelden unter: **www.StudySmarter.de/schule**

Richtig lernen, bessere Noten
7 Tipps wie's geht

1. **15 Minuten geistige Aufwärmzeit** Lernforscher haben beobachtet: Das Gehirn braucht ca. eine Viertelstunde, bis es voll leistungsfähig ist. Beginne daher mit den leichteren Aufgaben bzw. denen, die mehr Spaß machen.

2. **Ähnliches voneinander trennen** Ähnliche Lerninhalte, wie zum Beispiel Vokabeln, sollte man mit genügend zeitlichem Abstand zueinander lernen. Das Gehirn kann Informationen sonst nicht mehr klar trennen und verwechselt sie. Wissenschaftler nennen diese Erscheinung „Ähnlichkeitshemmung".

3. **Vorübergehend nicht erreichbar** Größter potenzieller Störfaktor beim Lernen: das Smartphone. Es blinkt, vibriert, klingelt – sprich: Es braucht Aufmerksamkeit. Wer sich nicht in Versuchung führen lassen möchte, schaltet das Handy beim Lernen einfach aus.

4. **Angenehmes mit Nützlichem verbinden** Wer englische bzw. amerikanische Serien oder Filme im Original-Ton anschaut, trainiert sein Hörverstehen und erweitert gleichzeitig seinen Wortschatz. Zusatztipp: Englische Untertitel helfen beim Verstehen.

5. **In kleinen Portionen lernen** Die Konzentrationsfähigkeit des Gehirns ist begrenzt. Kürzere Lerneinheiten von max. 30 Minuten sind ideal. Nach jeder Portion ist eine kleine Verdauungspause sinnvoll.

6. **Fortschritte sichtbar machen** Ein Lernplan mit mehreren Etappenzielen hilft dabei, Fortschritte und Erfolge auch optisch sichtbar zu machen. Kleine Belohnungen beim Erreichen eines Ziels motivieren zusätzlich.

7. **Lernen ist Typsache** Die einen lernen eher durch Zuhören, die anderen visuell, motorisch oder kommunikativ. Wer seinen Lerntyp kennt, kann das Lernen daran anpassen und erzielt so bessere Ergebnisse.

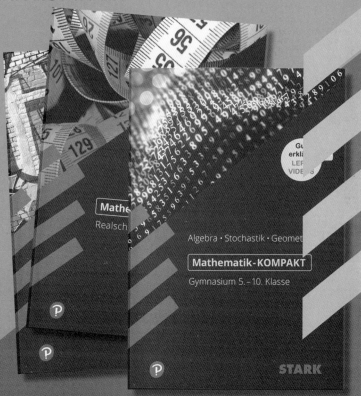

Kompakt zusammengefasst.
Wie dein Spickzettel
STARK KOMPAKT

Wir wissen, was Schüler brauchen.

 Pearson   www.stark-verlag.de   **STARK**

Witzige, interessante und schlaue Storys, Fakten und Spiele zum Thema Lernen und Wissen – gibt's nicht? Gibt's doch!

Auf **schultrainer.de** machen dich die Lernexperten vom STARK Verlag fit für die Schule.

Schau doch vorbei: **www.schultrainer.de**